Craving Vegan

Sam Turnbull

CRAVING VEGAN

101 Recipes to Satisfy Your Appetite the Plant-Based Way

appetite
by RANDOM HOUSE

Appetite by Random House® and colophon are registered trademarks
of Penguin Random House LLC.

Library and Archives Canada Cataloguing in Publication
is available upon request.
ISBN: 9780525610878
eBook ISBN: 9780525610885

Interior design: Talia Abramson
Interior photography: Tanya Pilgrim
Interior photography on pages v, viii, 3, 5, 21, and 265 by
Sam Turnbull and Adam Shirley

Printed in China

Published in Canada by Appetite by Random House®,
a division of Penguin Random House Canada Limited.

www.penguinrandomhouse.ca

10 9 8 7 6 5 4 3 2 1

For my perfect person, my husband, Adam.
Hi Adam! *waves*
Thank you for taste-testing every single recipe
in this book and swearing that each one was the
best dish you've ever had. Your support means
everything to me. I love you forever.

CONTENTS

Hi, Friends!

Welcome to my third cookbook! If you've cooked with me through my first two cookbooks, *Fuss-Free Vegan* and *Fast Easy Cheap Vegan*, I hope you're excited to amp it up and cook even more epic meals. If you're new, well hello there, good lookin'! I'm Sam, and I'm here to prove to you that vegan food doesn't have to suck. In fact, vegan food can be incredibly drool-worthy delicious. Come back for seconds, thirds, or even fourths, cherish every bite, and wonder why you don't always eat this way.

Sound like a bold claim? Well, it is. But I'm sticking to it. And I hope that after cooking through this book, you'll agree with me.

You see . . . I DIDN'T GO VEGAN BECAUSE I HATE FLAVOR.

I also didn't go vegan because I hate texture. I went vegan because of the animals, because of the planet, and because of my health.

That's probably not too surprising to you, yet when I share recipes for savory vegan meats or gooey vegan cheeses, I'm often met with comments like "If vegans don't want to eat meat, then they shouldn't eat things that replicate meat."

And I say, why not?

Like most vegans, I wasn't born and raised that way. I grew up enjoying meat, eggs, and dairy in a house that literally had animal heads on the walls! But when I decided to go vegan, I had to switch my diet and find foods that were just as satisfying to me. Now, I don't know a single person who went vegan because they hated the taste of animal products. Most people, just like me, go vegan for the animals, their health, and the planet.

So, it shouldn't be surprising that vegans, or people who are just trying to eat more plant-based, might miss some of the foods they grew up eating. So why not just eat animal meat? Because we don't miss the animal-killing part—we miss flavors and textures.

Some of us vegans might crave an animal product that we used to enjoy. And certain dishes can be associated with traditions or memories: Burgers and ribs at a barbecue. Soft-boiled eggs on Sunday mornings. Cheese and pâté at a cocktail party. Steak dinners for special celebrations. Chocolate and sweets at Christmas. Vegan versions of these dishes allow people to stick to their values and enjoy their favorite foods without harming any animals. So, you see, it's really win-win.

Some vegans or plant-based eaters out there are totally happy living on grain bowls, salads, and smoothies. And that's wonderful. But that's just not me. When I first went vegan, I tried to live off of those types of dishes. And, well . . . the truth is, I hated it. The food was tasty-ish, but it didn't have the kinds of tastes that I grew up loving. I missed the stretchy cheese pizzas, crunchy fried chicken, creamy alfredo pasta, and gooey chocolate desserts.

I couldn't go back to eating animal products after all I had learned about the animal agriculture industry, so I had to try to figure out this whole vegan food thing. That's when I began experimenting in the kitchen and trying to create recipes to appease my cravings. And it totally worked. I discovered that I could recreate textures and flavors that I desired, all while keeping it totally plant-based. I fell in love with creative vegan cooking. And with a little experimenting, I found that I could make any dish vegan—and not just vegan, but DELICIOUS!

Not only were the meals yummy and satisfying, but they actually tasted better than the original and made me feel awesome! I remember the joy I felt the first time I dove into a huge bowl of rich, creamy, luscious pasta that didn't taste like health food.

I wanted to document these recipes, so I began sharing them in 2013 on my blog, *It Doesn't Taste Like Chicken*, and I soon realized that I wasn't the only one craving these types of recipes. Millions of people from all over the world were craving drool-worthy vegan recipes, just like I was. Every time I posted a new recipe, I heard from people all over the world that I was helping satisfy their cravings (whether they were vegan or just trying to eat more plant-based). And that is how I fell in love with recipe writing. I knew that with every recipe I posted, I was helping people fall in love with vegan cooking, just like I did. I was helping the animals while making people happy. I mean, what more could a girl ask for?

I'm here to show you that you don't have to miss out on anything when eating plant-based. You can go vegan and eat great food too! Textures and flavors are not exclusive to animal products. They can be recreated in simple ways with seasoning and technique, or in fun, more experimental ways with some cool ingredients that might be new to your kitchen. Get ready to enjoy some incredible vegan eats and satisfy all your tastiest cravings.

What Craving Vegan Is All About

The idea for *Craving Vegan* came about when I was being interviewed with a few other awesome plant-based influencers. The host asked, "What does comfort food mean to you?" We all took turns answering. The first and second influencers answered similarly: it was all about the cozy foods you grew up with. And while I agreed, I had a slightly different thought when it was my turn to answer. To me, comfort food can be familiar, sure, but when I'm craving a certain type of meal, I'm more focused on the sensation that the meal satisfies. Am I craving something crunchy and salty? Rich and creamy? Fluffy and carby? Hot and spicy? Sweet and chocolaty?

Instead of dividing this book into common chapters like soups, salads, pastas, and desserts, I decided to divide it into cravings. When I ask myself what I want for dinner, I don't think soup, salad, or pasta. I think about what craving I want to satisfy.

⋟ HOW THIS BOOK WORKS ⋞

Craving Vegan is divided into nine chapters: eggy, carby, cheesy, creamy, crunchy, spicy, meaty, chocolaty, and sugary. Are you drooling yet?

Each chapter is filled with recipes to satisfy that specific craving. Some recipes will satisfy just the one craving, such as The Fluffiest Bread You've Ever Had (page 52), which is a carb lover's dream. There are also many recipes in this book that will satisfy more than one craving, such as the Crunch Wrap Superior (page 202), which you'll find in the meaty chapter but which is also carby, cheesy, crunchy, and spicy. (My stomach is already grumbling!)

As you flip through the chapters, you will see that each recipe has a legend of all the cravings it fulfills, so you can get your munch on!

Craving Ingredients

Many of the ingredients in the book will be familiar to you, and you'll likely have many in your kitchen already. In my first two books, I kept the ingredients fairly simple, but in this book, I'm introducing a few special ingredients in each chapter that may be new to your kitchen. Before we get into the recipes, I want to dive into each ingredient and share why I use it, along with some helpful tips. If you are unfamiliar with an ingredient or just want more info, make sure you give this chapter a read-through.

EGGY INGREDIENTS

Black Salt: Black salt is also called kala namak. Do not confuse it with any other kind of salt. Kala namak is very unique in that it tastes and smells just like eggs (it's actually kind of bizarre!). This is a common ingredient in Indian cuisine, so it is easy to find in international grocery stores or online, and it's usually very inexpensive. It's an absolute must for making vegan dishes taste eggy! Black salt is a little less salty than table salt, so I sometimes add both kinds of salt where needed. The flavor of black salt gets less intense when cooking, so if you find the flavor too strong, try cooking the dish a little longer, or if you find there isn't enough eggy flavor, add a pinch more!

Chickpea Flour: This flour is also called garbanzo bean flour. If your grocery store doesn't carry it, try a health-food store or international grocery store. I love using it to make my Chickpea Omelet (page 29). Just ensure that it cooks completely through because raw chickpea flour tastes bloody awful! When fully cooked it is super delicious and, bonus points, healthy too.

Split Mung Beans: You'll be able to find these at an international grocery store or online. Once mung beans are soaked and then blended, they make a batter that holds together similarly to eggs—very cool! That's why I love to use them in my Mung Bean Veggie Scramble (page 34) and my Folded Egg Sandwich (page 40).

CARBY INGREDIENTS

All-Purpose Flour: A staple in almost any kitchen, all-purpose flour yields a softer, fluffier result than whole wheat. If you prefer using whole wheat flour, you can substitute it in most recipes, but note that you may need to add more moisture to the dish and the result may be a bit denser. Because I'm not gluten-free, all-purpose flour is a staple for many of my favorite carby recipes. If you are gluten-free, recipes that call for just a small amount of flour (¼ cup/60 mL or less) will usually be successful with a gluten-free all-purpose flour blend. Recipes that require more flour than that do not always translate well with a gluten-free substitute. Look out for the gluten-free tag in each recipe to see which recipes are gluten-free or can be made gluten-free!

Instant Yeast & Active Dry Yeast: I know that working with yeast can be intimidating, which is why my yeast-free Sinful Cinnamon Buns (page 251) are so great! However, working with yeast is actually pretty easy. Just ensure you are using the correct yeast for the job. Instant yeast is better when you are aiming for a quick rise, such as in Nothing Beats Bao (page 49) or The Fluffiest Bread You've Ever Had (page 52). Active dry yeast needs a longer rise, which is why it's perfect for my No-Knead Crusty Bread (page 77).

Pasta, Gnocchi & Noodles: Most store-bought dried pastas are vegan (just check the ingredients list to be sure). Gnocchi is traditionally made with eggs, but a lot of store-bought brands are vegan—win-win! When it comes to noodles, there are many different egg noodles, so just make sure you check the ingredients to grab the vegan-friendly ones. Rice noodles are always a great choice!

CHEESY INGREDIENTS

Nutritional Yeast: A flaky, yellow dry good that kind of looks like fish food. (What? It's true!) This is not the same as the yeast used for bread making. It is an inactive yeast that has a cheesy, nutty taste, and it's a plant-based cooking staple. Many grocery stores carry it these days, but if yours doesn't, find it in health-food stores, in bulk-food stores, or online.

Raw Cashews: Cashews are mild in flavor, creamy, and easy to blend. This makes them the perfect nut for making vegan cheeses and creamy sauces. While roasted cashews are delicious for snacking and garnishing some dishes, they are not the best for making cheeses and sauces. Roasted cashews are dry, hard, and oily, so they do not break down and blend smoothly, so be sure to use raw cashews. They can be expensive, so I like to buy raw cashew pieces in bulk, which are usually cheaper. Since you are blending them anyway, you don't need them whole.

Cashew Cream

1:1 ratio (1 cup/250 mL raw cashews for 1 cup/250 mL water).

1. If you have a high-powered blender, skip to step 2. If you do not have a high-powered blender, you will first need to soften the cashews to ensure that they blend smoothly. To soften the cashews, place them in a medium pot and cover with water. Set over high heat and bring to a boil. Boil for 10 minutes or until the cashews have softened. Drain and rinse before using.

2. Add the cashews and 1 cup (250 mL) water to a blender and blend until completely smooth and creamy. Store in a sealed jar in the fridge for up to 5 days or in the freezer for up to 6 months. It may settle as it rests, so shake before using.

Raw Sunflower Seeds: My favorite seed to make nut-free cheeses. Some of my recipes call for raw cashews, but if you cannot consume cashews, raw sunflower seeds are a great substitute. They are a little firmer and tangier, so make sure you blend them as best you can. If you find the result to be a bit too tangy, add a touch of agave to cut the acidity.

Sunflower Cream

1:1 ratio (1 cup/250 mL raw sunflower seeds for 1 cup/250 mL water).

1. You will need to soften the sunflower seeds regardless of your blender. Soften the raw sunflower seeds by putting them in a medium pot and covering with water. Place over high heat and bring to a boil. Boil for 15 minutes, until the sunflower seeds have softened, then drain and rinse well.

2. Add the softened sunflower seeds and 1 cup (250 mL) water to a blender and blend until completely smooth and creamy. If needed, strain through a fine-mesh strainer, nut milk bag, or cheesecloth to remove any little bits. Store in a sealed jar in the fridge for up to 5 days or in the freezer for up to 6 months. It may settle as it rests, so shake before using.

Refined Coconut Oil: Coconut oil has the unique quality of being solid at room temperature, but it turns liquid at just 76°F (24°C). For this reason, it works beautifully to firm up cheeses or my Red Lentil Pâté (page 210), but it stays soft enough that it can be spreadable or melt when required. Make sure you use refined coconut oil, as it is completely scentless and flavorless. Unrefined coconut oil will add a strong coconut taste to your dishes, which is not the correct flavor when making cheeses. If you are allergic to coconut oil, try substituting it with vegetable shortening.

Sauerkraut: Not just a delicious condiment! Sauerkraut has a sour, kind of funky taste, so I love to use it in cheeses. I buy a jar of white sauerkraut and keep it in the back of the fridge. When measuring the sauerkraut, make sure to measure both the cabbage and the liquid.

Tapioca Starch (aka Tapioca Flour): Tapioca starch has this amazing ability to make sauces gooey and stretchy. Hellooo, cheese sauce. This is why it is key in several of my cheese recipes. Other starches and flours will thicken sauces, but only tapioca starch will give that cheesy stretch, so it's a pantry must! Your local grocery store should carry it, but if it doesn't, you'll be able to find it at bulk-food stores, health-food stores, or online grocers.

White Miso Paste: It's not just for miso soup! Miso is fermented soybeans. I love the umami taste it provides to recipes, making cheeses taste like they have aged for months (even though you just prepared them). Miso comes in various colors, and usually the darker it is, the stronger the flavor. White miso paste (which is actually light brown) is mild and my favorite to work with. In a pinch, you can sub it with another type of miso, but note that this might change the flavor and color of the dish.

CREAMY INGREDIENTS

Full-Fat Coconut Milk: This is the kind of coconut milk found in a can (not in the carton). It is super rich and high in fat, which makes it the perfect sub for heavy cream. I love the coconut flavor in many dishes, but if coconut isn't your thing, try a plant-based culinary cooking cream, cashew cream (page 9), or sunflower cream (page 9).

Plant-Based Milk: There are a TON of plant-based milk options today! (So many options that it makes me wonder why anyone would even want to drink cow's milk anymore!) When it comes to cooking with plant-based milk, my go-tos are oat or soy. That said, use whichever plant-based milk is

your favorite. Just make sure that your choice is unflavored (trust me, you do not want vanilla milk in your pasta), and I generally prefer the unsweetened varieties. For richer dishes, opt for plant milks that are higher in fat, such as coconut milk or cashew milk.

Roasted Red Bell Peppers: I call for roasted red bell peppers twice in this book—once for my Roasted Red Pepper Cheese Sauce (page 114) and again for my Velvety Roasted Red Pepper Pasta (page 133). They are smoky and savory in flavor, and they provide a beautiful color to these sauces. You can purchase store-bought jarred roasted red peppers, or do what I like to do and roast them yourself.

Roasting Red Bell Peppers

>>> You can roast red bell peppers a few different ways, depending on the equipment you have:

Step 1 (choose one method):

Gas stove method: If you have a gas stove, turn the flame on and place a whole red pepper directly on the burner grate above the flame (no pot or pan needed). Allow the pepper to cook until the skin turns black, then using tongs, rotate the pepper to cook the next side until the entire pepper is almost entirely blackened.

Oven method: Preheat your oven to 450°F (230°C) and lightly grease a baking sheet. Slice the peppers in half and remove the core and seeds. Place the peppers on the baking sheet sliced side down and roast for 15–20 minutes, until the skins have darkened and the peppers are tender.

Air-fryer method: Preheat your air fryer to 400°F (200°C). Slice the peppers in half and discard the core and seeds. Air-fry the peppers for 12–18 minutes, until the skins have darkened and the peppers are tender.

Step 2:

Place the hot blackened peppers in a bowl and cover with plastic wrap; alternatively, use a sealable food storage container. Allow the peppers to cool while covered. The steam will loosen the skin from the peppers. Once cool enough to handle, use your fingers to rub off the blackened skins and discard. Use a knife to trim away the stem and seeds and discard them as well. Do not wash the peppers or you will wash away most of the flavor. The roasted peppers are now ready to use and enjoy. Store in an airtight container in the fridge for up to 5 days or freeze for up to 6 months.

Vegan Butter: Also known as vegan margarine, there are many brands available these days. Some vegan butters are great for toast or frying foods but are maybe not the best for baking. When you're using a vegan butter for baking, make sure it works for that. My go-to brand for baking is Earth Balance Original Buttery Spread.

CRUNCHY INGREDIENTS

Corn Flakes: One of my favorite hacks for a crunchy coating that almost tastes like it's fried! Cornflakes are easy to find at any grocery store and can be subbed for panko if needed. Just crush them up a little before using them so they adhere better.

Ground Chia & Ground Flax: Both of these seeds will gel when mixed with warm water, so they make a great egg substitute. I use them in the crunchy chapter to help coatings stick. Ground chia is my preference because it gels almost instantly, but flax works as well—it just takes about 10 minutes to gel. I keep my ground chia and ground flax in the freezer so that they stay fresh.

Panko: Panko is a Japanese breadcrumb that is flaky and crunchier than Italian breadcrumbs. It makes a great coating when you want something to have a crunchy bite. You can find gluten-free panko when needed.

SPICY INGREDIENTS

Hot Peppers: Jalapeños are a commonly used pepper in North American cooking, but I also love Scotch bonnet peppers for their authentic Jamaican flavor and canned chipotle peppers in adobo sauce for their smokiness and depth. The seeds of any hot pepper are the spiciest part, so if you prefer less spice, discard the seeds before chopping up the pepper. When working with hot peppers, I recommend wearing gloves. There can be residual hot pepper oil on your fingers even after washing your hands, and you won't realize it's there until later that day when you rub your eye!

Hot Sauces: While I love to get creative with hot sauces, I've kept the hot sauces in this book simple, so they should be easy for everyone to find. I rely on sriracha (the cult classic hot sauce), Frank's RedHot Original Cayenne Pepper Sauce (perfect for barbecue vibes), and chili garlic sauce (also called sambal oelek).

Spicy Spices: Crushed red pepper flakes, cayenne, and black pepper are the spices I opt for in this book. In most of my recipes, I give a range for the spices so that you can add as much or as little as you prefer.

MEATY INGREDIENTS

Jackfruit: This fruit is very similar to the texture of shredded meat. How cool is that? (It's very cool!) Make sure you are purchasing young or green jackfruit in brine or in water (and not in syrup). When jackfruit is harvested young it has a savory taste, but when it's fully ripe it's very, very sweet. When cutting jackfruit, you will notice that it has a very tough core surrounded by softer, stringier flesh, and there are usually some seeds in there as well. All parts of the jackfruit are edible so you do not need to discard any of this. When prepping jackfruit for Root Beer Pulled Jackfruit (page 218) or Braised Cocoa Jackfruit Tacos (page 230), drain and rinse the jackfruit, then cut it into smaller pieces. Cut the slices from the core to the outer edge, which breaks up the tougher core as much as possible and makes for the best "pulled" texture. When using jackfruit in my Rack o' Ribs recipe (page 217), you will use only the softer, stringy part of the jackfruit, and you can either compost the leftover core and seeds or add them to one of the other jackfruit recipes.

Liquid Smoke: This bottle is filled with the condensation collected from a fire. It can be found near the barbecue sauces in your grocery store. This is potent stuff, and you won't need much to make your dish nice and smoky.

Mushrooms: With a meaty texture and an umami taste, mushrooms make a great meat substitute! I know some people don't love the texture of mushrooms but still enjoy the taste. If this is the case for you, I recommend trying some of my recipes where the mushrooms are more hidden, such as my Sausage Bolognese (page 200).

Red Beets: Deep red with earthy notes, beets add color and an iron-rich flavor to The Best Burger Ever (page 224), making it taste more like beef. Even if you don't like beets, I promise you won't be able to taste them in this recipe.

Smoked Paprika: One of my favorite spices for adding a smoky earthiness to a dish.

Soy Sauce: Soy sauce not only provides a salty flavor, but also has a strong umami taste (savory) and adds color. For all these reasons, it's a simple way to add some depth to a recipe. You can substitute soy sauce with liquid aminos or other gluten-free alternatives, such as tamari, if desired.

Tofu: If you do not love tofu, I bet you just haven't had it prepared well. If you are thinking of bland, squidgy white cubes, then I can guarantee you haven't had it prepared well! Tofu is bland and boring, and that's a wonderful thing because it can suck up any flavor you give it! You just need to season and cook it well and you can make beautiful dishes. Make sure to use the correct firmness of tofu that is listed in each recipe (extra-firm, firm, or soft) as this is crucial to getting the correct result.

Vital Wheat Gluten: Also called gluten flour, this flour is made from wheat by separating the starch from the gluten. Gluten is actually the protein in wheat, so this flour is very high in protein (usually 70% to 80% protein). Gluten is also what provides that stretch and chew that makes bread so nice. When you use it in combination with other ingredients, you can achieve an incredible, realistic meaty texture (I'm obsessed!). When you make vegan meats using vital wheat gluten, the finished product is called seitan. Of course, as the name would suggest, this is not gluten-free, and unfortunately there is no gluten-free alternative. You can find vital wheat gluten flour online or in health-food stores.

Vital Wheat Gluten Cleaning Tips

Vital wheat gluten is very sticky and can destroy dish brushes and cloths. So what I like to do is save old clothes, sheets, or towels that are too shabby to donate, and cut them into rags. I use these rags to clean up after preparing a seitan recipe and discard the rag once finished.

Walnuts: A great way to add some texture and richness to a meaty dish. Pecans work well as a substitute, or if you are nut-free you can try sunflower seeds or pepitas (shelled pumpkin seeds).

CHOCOLATY INGREDIENTS

Instant Espresso Powder: Espresso enhances the flavor of chocolate, so I always keep instant espresso powder on hand in my pantry. You won't taste the espresso (unless the flavor is intended), but you will taste amazing, awesome chocolate like never before!

Vegan Chocolate Chips: Some brands of chocolate chips are accidentally vegan, and others are purposefully vegan. If you are having difficulty finding chocolate chips, buy a bar of dark chocolate and use a big knife to chop it into chip-size pieces. I actually prefer chocolate chips made this way!

Vegan Dark Chocolate: Many brands of dark chocolate are vegan-friendly, but check the ingredients to make sure. I buy a big bar that I can break into pieces, both for snacking and cooking with.

SUGARY INGREDIENTS

Natural Peanut Butter: I always cook with natural peanut butter, which should include only one ingredient: peanuts (and maybe a bit of salt). The texture is more liquid and you will need to stir it. Tip: before you open a new jar of natural peanut butter, store it upside down to make it way easier to stir. Peanut butters that contain extra oils and sugars are basically icing. It's best to avoid these as they can make your baked goods dry and overly sweet.

Sugar: White, brown, and powdered sugar all have different purposes when baking, so make sure you use the sugar that is listed. In the US, some companies use bone char to refine sugar, technically making it not vegan. (As far as I know, this isn't common anywhere else in the world, so it's not likely a concern.) If this is a concern for you, you can look up information about the brand online, or organic sugar is always vegan-friendly.

Vegan Sprinkles & Food Coloring: I'm a total sucker for rainbow sprinkles or a fluffy pink icing! I think it's the kid in me. Some sprinkles are coated in shellac, which is made from insects (eww!). And some food coloring can be made using carmine, which comes from another kind of bug (double eww!). Just double-check the brand you're purchasing—a quick google will usually do the trick!

Craving Cooking Tools

If you're a new cook, you can probably get away with very simple cooking tools. Just a chef's knife, a cutting board, a good skillet, a large bowl, and a couple of spoons will get you very far! But if you are hoping to expand your kitchen and up your cooking game, some amazing tools can help you achieve the creamiest sauces, the meatiest meats, and the cheesiest cheeses! This is a list of my favorite cooking tools that help me get the best results.

Air Fryer: I'm not generally a fan of trendy kitchen gadgets, so when I heard about the air fryer, my first thought was that it was just another appliance that would probably take up too much space on the counter and collect dust. Well, I was wrong. I fell absolutely head over heels in love with my air fryer! If you crave crunchy deep-fried-tasting foods but aren't a fan of all that extra grease, then you NEED an air fryer. For all the crunchy recipes in this book, I provide instructions on pan-frying or oven baking, but I have also added cooking instructions for the air fryer where applicable.

Food Processor: Food processors are best used for more solid foods (while blenders are better for more liquid foods). A good food processor can help you whip cashews and coconut oil into a creamy, sticky cheese, knead dough, make seitan in a snap, and turn tofu and seasonings into a fluffy quiche filling. If you do not have a food processor, you can sometimes get away with mashing things by hand, but this tool will help you save a lot of time in the kitchen.

Grill Pan: OK, this isn't necessary, but it sure is fun. There is just something about grill marks on food that makes a dish seem extra delicious. If you're into making plant-based meats look even meatier, it's a great tool to have!

High-Powered Blender: If it's within your budget, I highly recommend treating yourself to a high-powered blender. I use mine almost daily! While a standard blender is great for blending soups and smoothies, it usually isn't strong enough to blend firmer ingredients like cashews and sunflower seeds into truly creamy cheeses or sauces (something you will see a lot of in this book). I use my blender to make everything from fondue, soups, and creamy sauces to mung bean eggs.

Steaming Pot: For my seitan recipes, including Ginger Beef (page 205), Seitan Steaks (page 207), Rack o' Ribs (page 217), Bangin' Bratwurst (page 222), and The Best Burger Ever (page 224), the vegan meats all need to be steamed to achieve a juicy, meaty, chewy texture. (I'm drooling already!) My pot set came with a stainless-steel steamer basket that sits on top of a large pot, which works wonderfully. You can get multiple layered steamer pots or bamboo steamer baskets so you can steam multiple batches at once. You can also find foldable steamer inserts designed to fit inside a pot but keep the food elevated above the water. Whatever steamer you have is great.

>>> For a DIY method, try putting a stainless-steel strainer in a pot that fits it, and top with a lid. Or puncture several holes in an aluminum pie plate and fit it over a pot with a lid. Save the pie plate and use it again and again (or until you upgrade to a steamer pot).

Flavor Cheat Sheet

'**I**'ve tested these recipes and seasoned them to perfection! Well, to my perfection anyway. While I recommend trying the recipe as written first before making any changes, I know everyone has slightly different taste preferences. So here is my little cheat sheet to help you correct your dish if you need to. Also, remember to take notes for the next time you cook the dish!

Too bland? Season with more salt. No, really. Salt is the ultimate flavor enhancer, so when something tastes bland, often all it needs is a little sprinkle of salt. If the dish is salty enough but still needs more oomph, try adding more of the spices and seasonings already used in the recipe.

Too intense? The first time you make a dish, always be sure to measure accurately. If you do not measure spices and seasonings correctly, it can be easy to over season a dish and make the flavor too intense. Try diluting the dish by adding more of the other ingredients in the recipe. Then serve with something bland like rice, pasta, potatoes, or bread.

Too salty? Add a few teaspoons of something acidic, such as vinegar or lemon juice. The acid will help cut the salt. Make a note to reduce the salt the next time you make the dish. Depending on the recipe, you could also try adding something creamy, such as cashew cream (page 9), full-fat coconut milk, or plain vegan yogurt, to help mask the saltiness.

Too spicy? Sweet, acidic, and creamy things all help cut through spice. So, depending on the recipe, try adding a teaspoon or two of sugar, maple syrup, agave, lemon juice, vinegar, or vegan butter, or a few tablespoons of vegan yogurt, cashew cream (page 9), or avocado. You can also serve the dish with something bland like rice, pasta, mashed potatoes, or bread.

Too mild? Add more of the spice that is already used in the dish, such as hot sauce, cayenne, or crushed red pepper flakes. Start with just ¼ tsp, adding more to taste.

Too sour? Try adding something sweet like a few teaspoons of agave, maple syrup, or sugar. You can also add a *tiny* pinch of baking soda, which will make it more alkaline.

Too sweet? Add something sour like a few teaspoons of lemon juice, lime juice, or vinegar.

Too bitter? Add some fats such as a tablespoon of oil, vegan butter, or avocado, and try adding a pinch of sweetness.

For those of us who love savory breakfasts, it can be a challenge to give up eggs. No more!! You can satisfy all of those eggy cravings with this chapter.

EGG

EGGY

Everything from runny eggy yolks to hearty breakfast sandwiches are all totally egg-free. The absolute key to getting that perfect eggy flavor is to use black salt (also called kala namak), so make sure you read about black salt on page 7 before plunging into this chapter.

Dippy Egg Yolk

This fan-favorite recipe will satisfy your eggy cravings in a flash! Just 5 minutes to make, only six ingredients, and completely cholesterol-free. I love to dip buttered slices of toast into this egg yolk for the most amazing breakfast treat, or you can drizzle the yolk sauce over any recipe where you want a little more egginess, such as my Egg Fried Rice (page 43) or No-Eggs Benny (page 31).

MAKES: ABOUT 1 CUP (250 ML) EGG YOLK SAUCE (4 SERVINGS)	COOK TIME: 5 MINUTES	TOTAL TIME: 5 MINUTES

1 cup (250 mL) water

1 Tbsp (15 mL) + 1 tsp cornstarch

2 Tbsp (30 mL) light oil (such as canola or vegetable)

2 tsp nutritional yeast

¾ tsp black salt (kala namak)

¼ tsp turmeric

OPTIONAL FOR SERVING

4 slices bread, toasted

Vegan butter for the toast

Salt and black pepper

1. In a small pot, whisk together the water and cornstarch. Now whisk in the oil, nutritional yeast, black salt, and turmeric.

2. Set over medium-high heat and whisk while it cooks. Cook for 3–5 minutes, until the dipping sauce thickens to an egg-yolk consistency. Serve hot with buttered toast, a sprinkle of salt, and a crack of pepper to taste.

>>> Make Ahead You can make this sauce ahead of time and, once cooled, store it in an airtight container in the fridge for up to 5 days. It will thicken as it cools, so you can gently reheat it and add a touch more water if needed. You can also freeze it in an airtight container for up to 6 months.

Spinach Quiche

CRAVINGS: EGGY, CARBY
GLUTEN-FREE, MAKE AHEAD

No eggs are in sight to make this vegan quiche. Instead I use my favorite friend: tofu. With black salt to get that eggy flavor, turmeric for the creamy yellow color, and spinach and other seasonings, this quiche is just like the traditional version, but better! This savory, fluffy, eggy treat makes for the loveliest brunch. You can also make it ahead of time, store it in the fridge uncooked, and then bake it in the morning.

MAKES: ONE 9-INCH (23 CM) QUICHE	**PREP TIME:** 10 MINUTES	**COOK TIME:** 40 MINUTES	**TOTAL TIME:** 50 MINUTES

1 Tbsp (15 mL) vegan butter or olive oil

1 small yellow onion, chopped

3 cloves garlic, minced

10.6 oz (300 g) frozen and thawed spinach, water squeezed out

1 block (12 oz/340 g) extra-firm tofu, drained

½ cup (125 mL) plant-based milk (such as oat or soy)

3 Tbsp (45 mL) nutritional yeast

1 Tbsp (15 mL) cornstarch

¾ tsp turmeric

¾ tsp black salt (kala namak)

½ tsp salt

Pinch of nutmeg

One 9-inch (23 cm) Perfect Flaky Pie Crust (page 79) or store-bought vegan pie crust (gluten-free if preferred)

1. Preheat your oven to 375°F (190°C).

2. Heat the butter in a skillet or nonstick frying pan over medium-high heat. Add the onions and garlic and sauté for about 5 minutes, until the onions turn translucent and begin to brown. Add the spinach and mix into the onions. Remove from the heat.

3. In a food processor, combine the tofu, plant-based milk, nutritional yeast, cornstarch, turmeric, black salt, salt, and nutmeg. Process, stopping to scrape down the sides, until it is as smooth as possible. Add the spinach mixture and pulse just a few times to mix in, using a spoon to mix if needed (do not blend the spinach).

4. Scoop the filling into the pie shell and spread it out evenly. Bake for 30–40 minutes, until the edges begin to brown and the center is set. Let cool for 10 minutes before slicing and serving.

>>> **Make Ahead** Prep the quiche so that the filling is spread in the pie shell. Cover with plastic wrap or similar covering and chill in the fridge overnight. Remove the plastic wrap and bake in the morning when ready to enjoy.

6 EGGY

26 EGGY

Chickpea Omelet

CRAVINGS: EGGY, CHEESY
GLUTEN-FREE, MAKE AHEAD

I stumbled upon this idea of using chickpea flour as an egg substitute for omelets, and I must say, it is completely brilliant! While it is not an exact dupe, this vegan omelet is close enough for me, and bonus points, it's full of protein and has zero cholesterol, making this a very healthy breakfast choice too! You can enjoy this omelet plain or try one of the four omelet fillings I've included my favorites! Feel free to play around with your own fillings too—omelets are great for using up leftover vegan cheese, vegan meats, and veg!

MAKES: 2 OMELETS	**PREP TIME:** 5 MINUTES (FOR THE PLAIN OMELET)	**COOK TIME:** 8 MINUTES (FOR THE PLAIN OMELET)

TOTAL TIME: 13 MINUTES (FOR THE PLAIN OMELET)

FOR THE PLAIN OMELET

1 cup (250 mL) chickpea flour (garbanzo bean flour; see note)

¼ cup (60 mL) nutritional yeast

1 tsp baking powder

1 tsp black salt (kala namak)

1⅓ cups (330 mL) plant-based milk (such as oat or soy)

1–2 Tbsp (15–30 mL) light oil (such as canola or vegetable), for frying

1 Tbsp (15 mL) chopped fresh herbs (such as chives, parsley, or basil), for garnish (optional)

OPTIONAL FILLINGS (CHOOSE 1)

CHEESE OMELET

½ cup (125 mL) Cheddary Coconut Cheese Sauce (page 111) or Roasted Red Pepper Cheese Sauce (page 114)

MUSHROOM OMELET

1 Tbsp (15 mL) vegan butter

½ yellow onion, thinly sliced

2 cloves garlic, minced or pressed

2 cups (500 mL) sliced mushrooms

Salt and black pepper, to taste

1 small handful fresh parsley or chives, chopped

Plain Omelet

1. In a medium bowl, whisk together the chickpea flour, nutritional yeast, baking powder, and black salt. Add the water and whisk well, making sure there are no lumps.

2. Heat 1 Tbsp (15 mL) oil in a good nonstick pan over medium heat. Pour in half of the chickpea batter and spread into a thin circle (it will puff up as it cooks). Cover with a lid and cook for 3–4 minutes, until the center is no longer wet. Carefully flip with a spatula and cover with the lid, cooking for another couple of minutes until completely cooked through. Make sure that the omelet is cooked and there are no wet spots, as uncooked chickpea flour tastes terrible. This may mean that the omelet is a bit more golden brown than a traditional egg omelet would be. Transfer the omelet to a plate and fold in half. Repeat with the remaining batter to make a second omelet. Enjoy alone with a garnish of fresh herbs or add any optional fillings.

OPTIONAL FILLINGS (prepare the fillings before cooking the omelet)

Cheese Omelet

1. Prepare your cheese sauce of choice. Prepare the omelet. When you flip the omelet over to cook the second side, spread about ¼ cup (60 mL) of the cheese sauce across the cooked surface of the omelet. When the bottom of the omelet is cooked, gently fold the omelet over so that the cheese is on the inside, and serve. Garnish with fresh herbs if desired.

RECIPE CONTINUES ⟶

1 Tbsp (15 mL) olive oil

1 lb (454 g) asparagus, tough ends trimmed

3 cloves garlic, minced

Salt and black pepper, to taste

3 Tbsp (45 mL) Super Quick Tofu Ricotta (page 106, optional)

1 Tbsp (15 mL) Sunflower Parmesan (page 107, optional)

PEPPERS & ONIONS OMELET

1 Tbsp (15 mL) olive oil

1 yellow or red onion, sliced

2 bell peppers (any color), sliced

3 cloves garlic, minced or pressed

Salt and black pepper, to taste

1 Tbsp (15 mL) chopped fresh herbs (such as chives, parsley, or basil), for garnish (optional)

Note

Chickpea flour is very affordable and should be available at your local grocery store, but if it isn't, you can easily find it at health-food stores, Indian grocery stores, or online grocery stores. It's pantry-friendly, so once you have a big bag you can whip up these amazing omelets all

Mushroom Omelet

1. Melt the butter in a nonstick pan or skillet over medium-high heat. Add the onions and garlic and sauté until the onions begin to soften. Add the mushrooms and sauté for another 5–10 minutes, stirring occasionally until the mushrooms darken and begin to release their juices. Remove from the heat and season with salt and pepper.

2. When your omelet is fully cooked, plate it and top one half with the sautéed mushrooms. Gently fold over the omelet so that the mushrooms are inside. Garnish with parsley or chives and extra black pepper.

Asparagus Omelet

1. Heat the olive oil in a skillet over medium-high heat. Add the asparagus and toss with tongs to evenly coat it in the oil. Cook for 4–8 minutes, stirring occasionally, until the asparagus is tender but still has bite. Add the garlic and cook for another 2 minutes, until the asparagus is tender throughout (but not mushy) and the garlic is cooked. Remove from the heat and season with salt and pepper.

2. When your omelet is fully cooked, plate it and top one half with the asparagus. Top with dollops of tofu ricotta or sunflower parmesan if desired. Gently fold over the omelet so that the asparagus is inside.

Peppers & Onions Omelet

1. Heat the oil in a large skillet over medium-high heat. Add the onions, peppers, garlic, salt, and pepper. Cook, stirring frequently, until the onions and peppers are cooked and beginning to brown, 5–10 minutes.

2. When your omelet is fully cooked, plate it and top one half with the peppers and onions. Gently fold over the omelet so that the peppers and onions are inside. Garnish with black pepper or fresh herbs if desired.

>>> **Make Ahead** Whip up this chickpea batter and store it in a jar in your fridge for up to 3 days. Just give it a good shake before using, then pour straight into the hot oiled pan.

No-Eggs Benny

An English muffin is layered with smoky seasoned sweet potato ham, a slice of eggy seasoned tofu, and a generous drizzle of hollandaise sauce. This epic breakfast will hit the spot every time! Feel free to add sautéed spinach, sliced tomatoes, chopped chives, or extra vegan egg yolk sauce (page 25), if you wish.

SERVES: 4	PREP TIME: 15 MINUTES	COOK TIME: 30 MINUTES	TOTAL TIME: 45 MINUTES

FOR THE SWEET POTATO HAM

- 1 Tbsp (15 mL) light oil (such as canola or vegetable)
- ½ Tbsp Dijon mustard
- ½ Tbsp soy sauce (gluten-free if preferred)
- ½ tsp liquid smoke
- ½ tsp onion powder
- ¼ tsp garlic powder
- 1 sweet potato, peeled and cut into eight ¼-inch-thick (6 mm) slices

FOR THE HOLLANDAISE

- ¼ cup (60 mL) vegan butter
- ¼ cup (60 mL) all-purpose flour (gluten-free if preferred)
- 1½ cups (375 mL) plant-based milk
- 1 Tbsp (15 mL) lemon juice
- 1 tsp Dijon mustard
- ¼ tsp black salt (kala namak)
- ¼ tsp salt
- ⅛ tsp turmeric

FOR THE TOFU EGG

- ¼ cup (60 mL) cornstarch
- ¼ cup (60 mL) nutritional yeast
- 1 tsp black salt (kala namak)
- 1 tsp onion powder
- 1 tsp garlic powder
- 1 block (16 oz/454 g) medium-firm tofu, drained and cut into 8 thick slices
- 1 Tbsp (15 mL) light oil (such as canola or vegetable)

FOR THE REST

- 4 English muffins, sliced in half and toasted (gluten-free if preferred)
- Chopped fresh chives or parsley, for garnish (optional)

1. Preheat your oven to 375°F (190°C). Line a baking sheet with parchment paper.

2. Make the sweet potato ham: In a small bowl, mix the oil, mustard, soy sauce, liquid smoke, onion powder, and garlic powder. Lay the sweet potato slices spaced out in a single layer on the prepared baking sheet. Generously brush each slice with the marinade. Bake for 10–20 minutes, until the edges of the sweet potatoes are golden brown and the potatoes are tender when pierced with a fork.

3. Make the hollandaise: Melt the butter in a saucepan over medium-high heat. Sprinkle the flour over the butter and whisk well to make a paste. Continuing to whisk, cook the flour mixture for another minute. Pour in the plant-based milk, lemon juice, mustard, black salt, salt, and turmeric, and whisk well to combine. Bring to a simmer and cook for about 5 minutes, whisking often, until the sauce thickens.

4. Make the tofu egg: In a medium bowl, whisk together the cornstarch, nutritional yeast, black salt, onion powder, and garlic powder. Dip each tofu slice into the cornstarch mixture to coat.

RECIPE CONTINUES ⟶

The tofu, sweet potato ham, and hollandaise sauce can all be made ahead of time and stored in the fridge for up to 4 days. You can gently reheat on the stove or in the microwave and assemble when ready to serve. While the tofu can be made ahead of time, it is best to make it fresh if you want the slightly crispy outside. The hollandaise sauce can be frozen in an airtight container for up to 6 months, but the other components do not freeze well.

5. Heat the oil in a nonstick pan over medium-high heat. Add the tofu slices, working in batches if needed, and fry each tofu slice until lightly golden on the bottom, 2–4 minutes. Gently flip the tofu slices and cook for another few minutes to brown the other side.

6. To assemble the benedicts, top each English muffin half with a slice of sweet potato ham, a tofu egg, and a drizzle of hollandaise, then garnish with chives or parsley if desired. Serve two English muffin halves per person.

Mung Bean Veggie Scramble

I love making this mung bean batter ahead of time. Then, when you're ready for a super easy, satisfying, protein-packed, fluffy, eggy breakfast, all you need to do is shake the batter and pour it into the pan! I prefer my scramble with sautéed veggies, but it's also great without. The texture is a little denser than scrambled eggs, but I actually prefer it.

SERVES: 4	PREP TIME: 5 MINUTES (PLUS SOAKING TIME)	COOK TIME: 10 MINUTES	TOTAL TIME: 15 MINUTES (PLUS SOAKING TIME)

FOR THE MUNG BEAN BATTER

½ cup (125 mL) dried split mung beans (moong dal), soaked overnight

⅔ cup (160 mL) plant-based milk (such as oat or soy)

½ tsp black salt (kala namak)

½ tsp salt, plus more to taste

¼ tsp onion powder

¼ tsp garlic powder

⅛ tsp black pepper, plus more to taste

⅛ tsp turmeric

FOR THE VEGGIES

1 Tbsp (15 mL) vegan butter or oil

1 red onion, thinly sliced

1 red bell pepper, chopped

3 cloves garlic, minced or pressed

1 Tbsp (15 mL) chopped fresh herbs (such as chives, parsley, or basil), for garnish (optional)

1. Make the mung bean batter: After soaking the mung beans overnight, drain them and rinse them well. Add the rinsed mung beans to a blender along with the plant-based milk, black salt, salt, onion powder, garlic powder, black pepper, and turmeric. Blend, stopping to scrape down the sides, until as smooth as possible.

2. Make the veggies: In a large nonstick skillet, melt the vegan butter over medium-high heat. Add the onions, peppers, and garlic. Sauté for about 5 minutes, stirring occasionally, until the veggies soften and just begin to brown.

3. Pour the mung bean batter evenly over the veggies, spreading the batter over the veggies evenly. Cook like a large pancake until the bottom is cooked, then flip and mix, using your spatula to break up the pancake into a scramble. Continue to cook and stir as needed, until all of the mung bean batter is fluffy, browned on the edges, and cooked thoroughly. Serve while hot and garnish with fresh herbs, salt, and pepper if desired.

>>> **Make Ahead** The mung bean batter can be made ahead of time and stored in a jar in the fridge for up to 4 days, or in an airtight container in the freezer for up to 3 months. Just shake well before using, then pour it straight into the pan. The veggies can be prepared fresh. You can also store leftover scramble in an airtight container in the fridge for up to 3 days.

One-Pan Breakfast Burritos

A lot of burrito recipes can be a bit complicated because you have to prepare a bunch of toppings and fillings separately, then assemble the burrito with the various fillings. This can be fun when you have a bit more time, but I simplified the recipe for an easier way to start the day. This breakfast burrito filling is whipped up in one pan, making it easy to prepare and quick to fill the burritos! Eggy, savory, perfectly seasoned, and filling, this is the perfect hearty, handheld breakfast.

MAKES: 8 BURRITOS	**PREP TIME:** 10 MINUTES	**COOK TIME:** 10 MINUTES	**TOTAL TIME:** 20 MINUTES

1 Tbsp (15 mL) light oil (such as canola or vegetable)

1 yellow onion, chopped

4 cloves garlic, minced or pressed

1 block (12 oz/340 g) extra-firm or firm tofu, drained and crumbled

1 can (19 oz/538 g) black beans, drained and rinsed

1½ cups (375 mL) chopped tomatoes (from 1 large tomato)

¼ cup (60 mL) nutritional yeast

1 tsp smoked paprika

1 tsp black salt (kala namak)

½ tsp salt

½ tsp ground cumin

½ tsp chili powder

½ tsp turmeric

¼ tsp cayenne (optional for spice)

2 avocados, chopped

½ cup (125 mL) chopped fresh cilantro

½–1 jalapeño, finely diced

8 large flour or corn tortillas (gluten-free if preferred)

1. Heat the oil in a large nonstick skillet over medium-high heat. Add the onions and garlic and sauté, stirring occasionally, until the onions turn translucent and begin to brown, about 5 minutes. Add the tofu, crumbling it into the pan with your fingers, followed by the black beans, tomatoes, nutritional yeast, paprika, black salt, salt, cumin, chili powder, turmeric, and cayenne (if using). Mix well so that the spices are evenly distributed, and heat through, about 5 minutes. Once everything is hot and mixed well, remove from the heat and stir in the avocados, cilantro, and jalapeños.

2. Assemble the burritos by adding a large scoop of the filling in the center of a tortilla. Fold each side of the tortilla over the filling, then roll up the burrito from the bottom to top so that the filling is enclosed inside the tortilla. You can optionally toast the burritos by heating a dry pan (no oil) over medium heat. Place the rolled-up burrito, seam side down, in the pan and toast until golden brown on the bottom—this will also seal it closed. Flip the burrito and toast the other side so it is also golden brown.

>>> Make Ahead The filling can be made ahead of time and the burritos can be assembled fresh. Prep the filling as written but omit the avocados, as they will turn brown. Allow the filling to cool, then store in an airtight container in the fridge for up to 4 days. Add the avocados just before serving, and wrap your burritos fresh.

Cheesy Broccoli Egg Cups

CRAVINGS: EGGY, CHEESY
GLUTEN-FREE, MAKE AHEAD

Ready for a cute breakfast treat? Try these egg cups! They are cheesy, fluffy, eggy, and stuffed with broccoli. They are like little quiches! My favorite thing about these cups is that you can prep them the night before and then just pop them in the oven to bake the next morning. Perfect for when company is visiting or as a gorgeous addition to your brunch spread.

MAKES: 10 EGG CUPS (4–5 SERVINGS)	**PREP TIME:** 10 MINUTES	**COOK TIME:** 40 MINUTES	**TOTAL TIME:** 50 MINUTES

1 Tbsp (15 mL) vegan butter or olive oil

1 yellow onion, chopped

6½ oz (184 g) broccoli, finely chopped (3 cups/750 mL chopped)

3 cloves garlic, minced

1 block (16 oz/454 g) firm tofu, drained

¼ cup (60 mL) nutritional yeast

2 Tbsp (30 mL) cornstarch

2 tsp white miso paste

½ tsp black salt (kala namak)

½ tsp salt

¼ tsp turmeric

¼ tsp black pepper

1–3 Tbsp (15–45 mL) plant-based milk (such as oat or soy), if needed

1. Preheat your oven to 350°F (175°C). Use a 12-count silicone muffin tray or line a standard metal muffin tray with parchment cupcake liners.

2. Heat the vegan butter in a skillet over medium-high heat. Add the onions, broccoli, and garlic and sauté, stirring occasionally, until the veggies soften and begin to brown, about 5 minutes. Remove from the heat and set aside. The broccoli should be partially cooked but still have a bit of bite, as it will continue to cook in the oven.

3. In a food processor, combine the tofu, nutritional yeast, cornstarch, white miso paste, black salt, salt, turmeric, and pepper and blend until completely smooth, stopping to scrape down the sides as needed. If your mixture is a bit dry, add the plant-based milk 1 Tbsp (15 mL) at a time, to reach a nice smooth consistency.

4. Add the broccoli and onions to the food processor and pulse, just a couple of times, to mix the broccoli in (do not fully blend the broccoli into the tofu). You can also just mix the tofu and broccoli together in a bowl if you prefer.

5. Fill the prepared muffin tray with the tofu broccoli mixture. The batter will not rise, so you can fill the muffin cups to the top. Bake for 25–30 minutes, until the tops are golden. Remove from the oven and let cool for 10 minutes before serving.

>>> Make Ahead You can prepare the tofu broccoli mixture and fill the muffin cups. Cover and chill in the fridge overnight and then bake in the morning. You can also allow the fully cooked egg cups to cool, then store them in an airtight container in the fridge for up to 4 days.

Folded Egg Sandwich

CRAVINGS: EGGY, CARBY, CHEESY
GLUTEN-FREE, MAKE AHEAD, FREEZER-FRIENDLY

I love a good breakfast sandwich, and this one is so satisfying and so easy to whip up that it has become a new staple in my house. The folded egg batter is the same as the batter in the mung bean scramble, except here we are using it to make the most epic sandwich! I like stuffing my folded egg with vegan cheese in the center as a fun surprise, but this is totally optional. You could also just add the vegan cheese on top of the sandwich or omit it. Feel free to play around with different sandwich toppings as well!

SERVES: 4	PREP TIME: 5 MINUTES (PLUS SOAKING TIME)	COOK TIME: 10 MINUTES	TOTAL TIME: 15 MINUTES (PLUS SOAKING TIME)

FOR THE FOLDED EGG

1 cup (250 mL) dried split mung beans (moong dal), soaked overnight

1⅓ cups (330 mL) plant-based milk (such as oat or soy)

1 tsp black salt (kala namak)

1 tsp salt

1 tsp onion powder

½ tsp garlic powder

¼ tsp black pepper

¼ tsp turmeric

FOR THE SANDWICHES

1–3 Tbsp (15–45 mL) vegan butter or oil, for frying

½ cup (125 mL) Cheddary Coconut Cheese Sauce (page 111) or store-bought vegan cheese (optional)

4 bagels, sliced in half and toasted if desired (gluten-free if preferred)

1 avocado, mashed

1 tomato, sliced

Hot sauce (optional)

1. Make the folded egg: Drain and rinse the soaked mung beans. Place the rinsed mung beans in a blender with the plant-based milk, black salt, salt, onion powder, garlic powder, pepper, and turmeric. Blend until completely smooth, stopping to scrape the sides as needed.

2. Make the sandwiches: Heat 1 Tbsp (15 mL) vegan butter in a large nonstick pan over medium-high heat. Pour about ⅔ cup (160 mL) of the batter in the pan and gently spread the batter out to make a large pancake, about ¼ inch (6 mm) thick. Do not make the pancake too thin or it will be difficult to flip. Let it cook until it is mostly cooked through, is lightly browned on the bottom, and releases from the pan. Flip the pancake over and continue to cook the other side. If you want a stuffed folded egg, you can optionally put about 2 Tbsp (30 mL) cheddary coconut cheese sauce in the center of the pancake. Now use your spatula to fold the sides of the pancake into the center and over the cheese, making the pancake a square shape. Repeat to make four folded eggs in total.

3. Spread the bottom half of the bagels with mashed avocado and a slice or two of tomato. Top with the folded egg, a dash of hot sauce if desired, and the top of the bagel. Enjoy!

>>> **Make Ahead** Make the folded egg batter and store in a jar in the fridge for up to 4 days, or in an airtight container in the freezer for up to 3 months. Shake well before using, then pour it straight into the pan. Cooked folded eggs (with or without the vegan cheese) can also be made ahead of time, allowed to cool, and then stored in an airtight container in the fridge for up to 3 days or in the freezer for up to 3 months. Assemble the sandwiches fresh.

Note

If you find it difficult to fold the mung bean egg, just cut the cooked pancake into slices instead and stack them on your sandwich.

Egg Fried Rice

Now for a non-breakfast eggy-type recipe—egg fried rice! The secret to fried rice is to use cooked and completely cooled rice (which is also the perfect way to use up leftover rice). Our good friend tofu is used to make the egg portion, and you can use whatever veggies you have on hand, making this recipe a great fridge-cleaner-outer.

SERVES: 4	PREP TIME: 15 MINUTES	COOK TIME: 20 MINUTES	TOTAL TIME: 35 MINUTES

FOR THE VEGAN SCRAMBLED EGG

1 Tbsp (15 mL) vegan butter or light oil (such as canola or vegetable)

½ block (6 oz/170 g) firm or medium-firm tofu

1 Tbsp (15 mL) nutritional yeast

½ tsp black salt (kala namak)

½ tsp onion powder

½ tsp garlic powder

¼ tsp turmeric

FOR THE FRIED RICE

1 Tbsp (15 mL) light oil (such as canola or vegetable)

2 cups (500 mL) veggies of choice (such as peeled diced carrots, frozen peas, diced bell peppers, or corn kernels)

1 yellow onion, chopped

4 cloves garlic, minced or pressed

3 cups (750 mL) cooked and cooled rice (leftover rice works great!)

2 Tbsp (30 mL) soy sauce (gluten-free if preferred)

1 tsp sesame oil

3 green onions, chopped

1. Make the vegan scrambled egg: Melt the vegan butter in a medium skillet or nonstick frying pan over medium-high heat. Add the tofu and break apart with your spatula. Don't crumble the tofu too much; you want some nice pieces of tofu in there so that the egg flavor and texture won't blend into the rice too much. Sprinkle with the nutritional yeast, black salt, onion powder, garlic powder, and turmeric and stir to combine and evenly coat. Remove from the heat and set aside.

2. Make the fried rice: Heat the oil in a large wok or nonstick pan over medium-high heat. When hot, add the veggies, onions, and garlic. Sauté until the veggies are cooked through and tender, 5–10 minutes. Add the rice, soy sauce, and sesame oil and stir well to combine. Once heated through, add the vegan scrambled egg and gently stir to mix in. Remove from the heat and garnish with the green onions.

>>> **Make Ahead** Allow the fried rice to cool completely, then store in an airtight container in the fridge for up to 4 days or in the freezer for up to 3 months.

BY

>>> Fluffy, crusty, pillowy, doughy—this is the chapter for those of us who are carb lovers (aren't we all!?). OK, so technically most foods are made up of a balance of carbohydrates, proteins, and fats, but we are focusing solely on the most carby of foods. I'm talking the fluffiest bread you've ever tasted, stuffed pasta shells, herby potato wedges, and hearty risotto, to name only a few.

Potato-Lover Pierogies

Pierogies are often made with eggs, butter, sour cream, and cheese. In my version, you taste all the richness and cheesiness while keeping it totally vegan. These potato dumplings are a bit time-consuming to make, but a fun project to try on a weekend. They also freeze beautifully, so I love having them ready to go in the freezer and being able to pull a few out later in the week for a quick potato-y, cheesy, scrumptious meal!

MAKES: 30–35 PIEROGIES (7–8 SERVINGS)	**PREP TIME:** 30 MINUTES (PLUS RESTING TIME FOR THE DOUGH)	**COOK TIME:** 35 MINUTES

TOTAL TIME: 65 MINUTES (PLUS RESTING TIME FOR THE DOUGH)

FOR THE DOUGH

2½ cups (625 mL) all-purpose flour

1 cup (250 mL) plant-based milk (such as oat or soy)

2 Tbsp (30 mL) vegan butter, melted

½ tsp salt

FOR THE FILLING

1 lb (454 g) russet potatoes, peeled and quartered

¼ cup (60 mL) nutritional yeast

¼ cup (60 mL) plant-based milk (such as oat or soy)

1 Tbsp (15 mL) white miso paste

FOR THE CARAMELIZED ONIONS (OPTIONAL FOR SERVING)

2 Tbsp (30 mL) vegan butter

2 yellow onions, thinly sliced

4 cloves garlic, minced or pressed

½ tsp salt

½ tsp white sugar

FOR SERVING (OPTIONAL)

Vegan sour cream

Vegan yogurt

Applesauce

Chopped fresh parsley

Make the Dough

1. Dough Hook Method: If you have a stand mixer with a dough hook or a food processor with a dough blade, you can prepare the dough using one of them. Place the flour, plant-based milk, vegan butter, and salt in your mixer bowl or food processor and mix, scraping the sides as needed, until a dough forms. Continue to mix with the dough hook or blade to knead the dough until it is nice and smooth and elastic. Wrap in plastic wrap and let rest in the fridge for 30 minutes while you prepare the rest of the ingredients.

Bowl Method: In a large bowl, mix together the flour, plant-based milk, vegan butter, and salt. Transfer to a clean work surface and knead it by hand for about 5 minutes until a nice dough forms, sprinkling with a bit of flour if needed to prevent sticking. Wrap in plastic wrap and let rest in the fridge for 30 minutes while you prepare the rest of the ingredients.

Make the Filling

2. Place the potatoes in a large pot and cover with water. Bring to a boil and continue to cook until the potatoes are fork-tender, 10–15 minutes. Remove from the heat and drain the water off the potatoes, keeping them in the pot. Add the nutritional yeast, plant-based milk, and miso paste. Mash and mix together, then cover and set aside.

RECIPE CONTINUES ⟶

Make the Pierogies

3. Lightly flour a clean work surface and roll the dough out to about ⅛ inch (3 mm) thick. Use a round 3-inch (8 cm) cookie cutter or a glass turned upside down to cut out dough circles. Add ½ Tbsp potato mixture to each circle, then fold the circles in half over the potato filling to make a crescent-moon shape. Pinch the edges together, making sure they are crimped well. Collect the scrap dough and reroll it to make more pierogies until all of the dough and filling are used up. Use right away or freeze for later (see the Make Ahead note).

Cook the Pierogies

4. Bring a large pot of water to a boil. Add the fresh or frozen pierogies, working in batches of no more than 10 to ensure they have lots of room to cook. Once the pierogies float to the surface, allow them to cook about 3 minutes more if cooking from fresh, or 5 minutes more if cooking from frozen to ensure they are cooked through. Remove with a slotted spoon and set aside on a plate.

Make the Caramelized Onions

5. Melt the vegan butter in a skillet or pot with a lid over medium-high heat. Add the onions, garlic, salt, and sugar. Cover and cook the onions, adjusting the heat as needed to keep them from burning. After about 5 minutes, the onions should be soft and translucent. Remove the lid and continue to cook the onions, stirring regularly to stop them from burning, about 10 minutes more. You can enjoy the boiled pierogies now with the caramelized onions, or you can fry the pierogies.

Fry the Pierogies (Optional)

6. Push the onions to the side of the pan. If the pan appears dry, add another pat of vegan butter to the pan. Add the drained pierogies and fry them for a few minutes per side until browned and crisp. Stir in the onions and serve with sauces or garnishes as desired.

>>> **Make Ahead** Store the cooked and cooled pierogies in an airtight container in the fridge for up to 3 days. If you'd like to freeze them, prepare the pierogies following steps 1–3, then spread them in a single layer on a parchment-lined baking sheet and freeze overnight. The next day, transfer the pierogies to an airtight container and return to the freezer for up to 3 months.

Nothing Beats Bao

On Sundays, my husband and I love to go out to a local pub and have a beer and a bao. Bao (pronounced "bow") are sweet, fluffy, pillowy buns that originate from Chinese cuisine. They are often filled with different types of meat or vegetables. In my version, I fill the bao buns with sweet, salty, spicy mushrooms and top them with crunchy peanuts—is there anything better? Due to the pandemic, our favorite pub wasn't always open, so I learned how to make bao at home so we could continue our tradition. These bao take a little work, but the results are so worth it! I like to make the bao buns and store them in the freezer so that Sunday's bao and beer are ready to go! You can enjoy the bao buns alone as a fluffy, carby snack or make the mushroom filling to make them more of a meal.

MAKES: 12–16 BAO	**PREP TIME:** 20 MINUTES (PLUS 1½ HOURS RISING TIME)	**COOK TIME:** 40 MINUTES

TOTAL TIME: 1 HOUR (PLUS 1½ HOURS RISING TIME)

FOR THE BAO BUNS

1 cup (250 mL) warm plant-based milk (think bath-water temperature)

¼ cup (60 mL) white sugar

1 Tbsp (15 mL) instant yeast

2½ cups (625 mL) all-purpose flour (use bleached flour if you want completely white buns)

½ tsp baking powder

¼ tsp salt

Light oil (such as vegetable or canola) or cooking spray, for brushing bao

FOR THE MUSHROOM FILLING (OPTIONAL)

¾ cup (185 mL) vegetable broth

2 Tbsp (30 mL) all-purpose flour

2 Tbsp (30 mL) soy sauce

1 Tbsp (15 mL) hoisin

1 Tbsp (15 mL) rice vinegar

1–2 tsp chili garlic sauce (optional for spice)

Pinch of cinnamon

1 Tbsp (15 mL) sesame oil

Make the Bao Buns

1. In a large measuring cup or medium bowl, mix together the plant-based milk, sugar, and yeast. Cover with a clean dish towel and set aside for 5–10 minutes. After resting, it should be very foamy on top. (If it isn't foamy, your yeast is likely too old, so you should purchase new yeast and try again.)

2. In a large bowl, whisk together the flour, baking powder, and salt. Add the yeast mixture and mix into a dough. On a clean work surface, knead the dough for about 5 minutes (you shouldn't need to add any flour, but if you do, add only a little so the dough doesn't get too dry). You can alternatively knead the dough in a stand mixer with a dough hook.

3. Lightly grease a clean large bowl (I generally clean and dry the bowl I was just using to save on dishes). Add the dough ball and turn it to coat it in oil. Cover with a clean dish towel and let rise somewhere warm for about 1 hour, until doubled in size. (The oven with just the light turned on is a great spot to rise dough.) If you plan on making the mushroom filling, I suggest doing this now while the dough is rising (see below).

4. Once the dough has risen, punch it down. Take the dough and roll it into a long rope. Cut the rope into 12–16 even-size balls. Take one ball at a time and roll it into a circle about 4 inches (10 cm) in diameter. Continue with the next steps.

RECIPE CONTINUES ⟶

6 green onions, chopped
   (light parts and dark parts
   separated)

2 cloves garlic, minced or
   pressed

1 lb (454 g) cremini mushrooms,
   sliced

FOR ASSEMBLY (OPTIONAL)

1 medium carrot, peeled and
   grated

1 handful fresh cilantro, coarsely
   chopped

½ cup (125 mL) roasted, salted
   peanuts, coarsely chopped

>>> **Make Ahead** Steamed bao can be stored in the fridge without filling for 3–4 days. Allow the bao to cool completely, then store in an airtight container with a paper towel to absorb extra moisture. Enjoy cold, or reheat by steaming again for a few minutes. Bao also freeze very well. To do so, first steam the bao and then let them cool completely. Spread the bao in a single layer on a baking sheet and then freeze overnight. Once frozen, store the bao in a freezer-friendly container for up to 3 months. Reheat by steaming again for a few minutes until warmed through.

5. Cut 4-inch (10 cm) squares of parchment paper, one for each of your bao circles. Place each dough circle on a square of parchment paper, then lightly brush the tops with the oil or use cooking spray. Fold each circle in half onto itself and gently press together to make the two sides stick into a half-circle shape. Place each bao on a baking sheet or cover with plastic wrap. Allow to rise for 15–30 minutes, until poofy.

6. When ready to steam the bao, add several inches of water to a large pot with a steamer basket and bring to a simmer. Add a few of the bao on their parchment-paper squares to the steamer in a single layer, arranging each bao about 1 inch (2.5 cm) apart, and cover and steam for 10 minutes. You will need to work in batches as you will be able to fit only about four bao at a time (depending on how big your steamer basket is). Remove from the heat and allow to cool for about 3 minutes. Enjoy the bao plain or fill them with the prepared mushroom filling (see assembly below).

Make the Mushroom Filling

7. In a measuring cup or small bowl, whisk together the vegetable broth, flour, soy sauce, hoisin, rice vinegar, chili garlic sauce (if using), and cinnamon. Set aside.

8. Heat the sesame oil in a large skillet over medium-high heat. Add the light parts of the green onions (white and light-green parts) and the garlic. Sauté for 3–5 minutes until the onions begin to soften. Add the mushrooms and reduce the heat to medium. Cook until the mushrooms have darkened and released their juices, 5–10 minutes, stirring occasionally.

9. Whisk the sauce again as it may have settled while resting, then pour it into the mushrooms. Bring to a simmer and cook until the sauce has thickened, another 3–5 minutes. Set aside until you are ready to assemble the bao.

Assemble the Bao

10. Take a freshly steamed bao and gently pull the two sides apart. Fill each bao with about 2 Tbsp (30 mL) of the mushroom filling, some grated carrot, cilantro, chopped peanuts, and the dark-green parts of the green onions.

The Fluffiest Bread You've Ever Had

This vegan milk bread is lightly sweet, with a sesame and salt topping. It's the ultimate way to satisfy your carby cravings. This recipe makes one loaf, but I normally double this to make two loaves, because one is usually not enough! You have been warned.

MAKES: 1 LOAF **PREP TIME:** 20 MINUTES (PLUS 2 HOURS RISING TIME) **COOK TIME:** 20 MINUTES

TOTAL TIME: 40 MINUTES (PLUS 2 HOURS RISING TIME)

FOR THE BREAD

- ¾ cup (185 mL) plant-based milk (such as oat or soy), warmed (think bath-water temperature)
- 3 Tbsp (45 mL) white sugar
- 1½ tsp instant yeast
- 2 cups (500 mL) all-purpose flour
- 1 Tbsp (15 mL) melted vegan butter
- ¾ tsp salt

FOR THE TOPPING

- 1–2 tsp plant-based milk (such as oat or soy), for brushing
- 1–2 tsp sesame seeds, for topping (optional)
- ½ tsp flaky salt, for topping (optional)
- 1 Tbsp (15 mL) melted vegan butter

1. In a large bowl, whisk together the plant-based milk, sugar, and yeast. Cover the bowl with a clean dish towel and let sit for 10 minutes. The mixture should be very foamy. (If it isn't foamy, your yeast is likely too old, so you should purchase new yeast and try again.)

2. Add the flour, melted vegan butter, and salt and stir in until a soft dough is formed. Lightly flour a clean work surface and turn the dough onto the surface, adding more flour as needed to keep the dough from sticking to your hands and your work surface. Knead the dough for 3–5 minutes, until the dough bounces back quickly when poked.

3. Lightly oil a large clean bowl. Put the dough into the greased bowl and turn the dough ball in the bowl to coat in oil. Cover the bowl with a clean dish towel. Let rise somewhere warm for 1 hour, until doubled in size. The oven with just the light turned on is a great place to rise dough.

4. Once the dough has doubled in size, you can punch it down and remove it from the bowl. Divide the dough into three even pieces and form it into three balls. Line a 4 × 8-inch (10 × 20 cm) loaf pan with parchment paper, or grease the pan well. Place the three balls in a row in the loaf pan. Cover with a clean dish towel and let rise somewhere warm for 1 hour, until doubled in size.

5. When ready to bake your bread, preheat your oven to 350°F (175°C). Generously brush the top of the risen bread with the plant-based milk, then sprinkle all over with the sesame seeds and flaky salt, if using. Bake until dark golden on top, about 20 minutes.

6. Allow the bread to cool for at least 15 minutes before removing from the pan. Then allow to cool another 15 minutes on a plate or rack before slicing. When ready to enjoy, brush the top of the loaf with the melted vegan butter. The bread will be the fluffiest and most delicious while still warm, so I recommend having a slice or two before storing.

>>> *Make Ahead* Store leftovers wrapped in a plastic bag, wax paper, or a clean dish towel at room temperature for up to 3 days. To freeze the bread, allow to cool completely before storing in a silicone or plastic bag and freezing for up to 6 months.

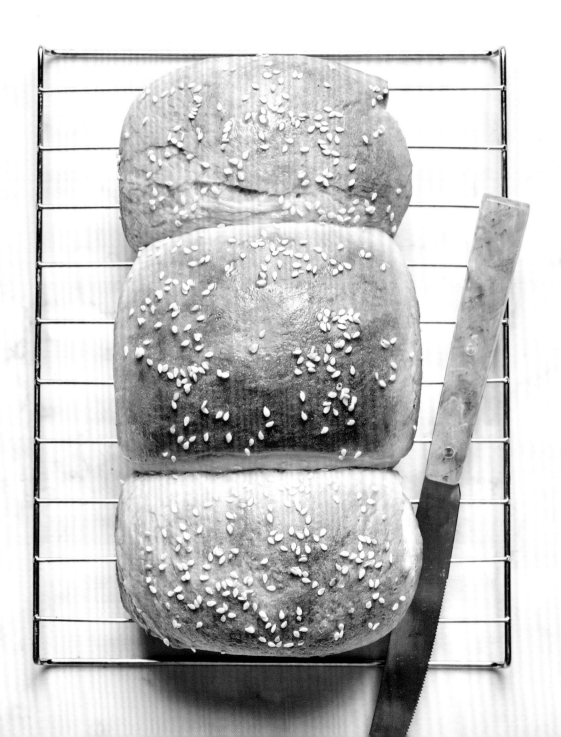

Saucy Spaghetti Bake

Uncooked spaghetti is added to a baking dish along with water, tomato sauce, and seasonings, and then it's baked. Yes, you read that right: the spaghetti bakes in the oven! (How cool is that?) When you boil spaghetti, the water that you drain away has a ton of starch in it, but in this recipe the starch has nowhere to escape, so it cooks into the sauce and makes it extra luscious and creamy! Topped with a quick homemade alfredo sauce, this easy recipe will become a new weeknight staple.

SERVES: 6-8	PREP TIME: 10 MINUTES	COOK TIME: 55 MINUTES	TOTAL TIME: 1 HOUR 5 MINUTES

FOR THE SPAGHETTI

1 lb (454 g) uncooked spaghetti (see note)

1 jar (22 fl oz/650 mL) prepared tomato sauce or 1 batch Simple Tomato Sauce (page 165)

3½ cups (875 mL) water

¼ cup (60 mL) tomato paste

1 yellow onion, chopped

4 cloves garlic, minced or pressed

1 tsp dried basil leaves

1 tsp dried oregano leaves

¾ tsp salt

¼ tsp black pepper

¼ tsp crushed red pepper flakes (optional)

FOR THE CREAMY ALFREDO SAUCE

¼ cup (60 mL) vegan butter

2 cloves garlic, minced or pressed

¼ cup (60 mL) all-purpose flour

1½ cups (375 mL) plant-based milk (such as oat or soy)

1 Tbsp (15 mL) nutritional yeast

½ tsp salt

½ tsp dried basil leaves

½ tsp onion powder

¼ tsp black pepper

1. Preheat your oven to 375°F (190°C).

2. Make the spaghetti: In a large 4½-quart (4.5 L) casserole dish, combine the spaghetti, tomato sauce, water, tomato paste, onions, garlic, basil, oregano, salt, pepper, and crushed red pepper flakes (if using). Use tongs to mix everything until combined. Cover and bake for 40 minutes, stopping halfway through to stir and make sure the pasta isn't sticking to the bottom of the pan.

3. Make the alfredo sauce: While the spaghetti is baking, melt the vegan butter in a saucepan over medium-high heat. Add the garlic and cook for about 1 minute while stirring. Sprinkle with the flour and stir to make a paste. Cook the flour paste for 1–2 minutes while stirring frequently to cook the flour. Whisk in the plant-based milk, nutritional yeast, salt, basil, onion powder, and pepper. Bring to a simmer and cook until the sauce is nice and thickened, about 5 minutes. Remove from the heat.

4. After the pasta has baked for the 40 minutes, remove the lid and spread the alfredo sauce over the pasta. Return to the oven and bake another 10–15 minutes, until bubbly. Allow the pasta to cool for 10 minutes before serving.

>>> **Make Ahead** I prefer this pasta fresh, but if you have leftovers, allow the dish to cool before covering and storing in the fridge for up to 3 days.

Note

I like to make this recipe with a regular wheat pasta. Some gluten-free pastas might work as well, but because the cooking times and starch contents vary, the results may differ.

Buttery Soft Pretzels

These golden, soft, and chewy pretzels satisfy carby cravings like no other! Enjoy these salty, buttery treats with mustard, dip them into Ooey Gooey Fondue-y (page 85), or serve them with Beer & Cheese Soup (page 90). However you serve them, you'll be coming back for seconds!

MAKES: 8 PRETZELS	**PREP TIME:** 30 MINUTES (PLUS 1 HOUR RISING TIME)	**COOK TIME:** 20 MINUTES

TOTAL TIME: 50 MINUTES (PLUS 1 HOUR RISING TIME)

FOR THE PRETZEL DOUGH

3 Tbsp (45 mL) white sugar (sub maple syrup or agave if preferred)

2¼ tsp (1 packet) active dry yeast

1 cup (250 mL) warm water (think bath-water temperature)

2½ cups (625 mL) all-purpose flour

1 Tbsp (15 mL) melted vegan butter

FOR THE BAKING SODA BATH

4 cups (1 L) water

¼ cup (60 mL) baking soda

FOR GARNISH

1–2 Tbsp (15–30 mL) rock salt

Melted vegan butter

Mustard

1. Make the pretzels: In a large bowl, whisk together the sugar and yeast. Add the warm water and mix. Let sit for 10 minutes. The mixture should be very foamy. (If it isn't foamy, your yeast is likely too old, so you should purchase new yeast and try again.)

2. Add the flour and melted vegan butter to the yeast mixture and stir in until a shaggy dough forms. Lightly flour a clean work surface and turn the dough onto the surface. Knead the dough for 3–5 minutes, until it comes together into a nice firm ball of dough.

3. Lightly grease a large clean bowl with more melted vegan butter. Put the dough into the greased bowl and cover with a clean dish towel. Let rise somewhere warm for 1 hour, until doubled in size. (The oven with just the light turned on is a great place to rise dough.)

4. Once the dough has doubled in size, punch it down and remove it from the bowl. Cut into eight even pieces. Take one piece and roll into a rope about 17 inches (43 cm) long. Twist the rope to form a pretzel shape. Repeat with the remaining pieces of dough.

5. Preheat your oven to 400°F (200°C). Line two baking sheets with parchment paper.

6. Make the baking soda bath: Heat the water in a medium pot until it reaches a light simmer. Stir in the baking soda—it will foam a lot. Place a pretzel on a slotted spatula, then dip it into the baking soda bath for 5 seconds. Now place the dipped pretzel on the prepared baking sheet and sprinkle with rock salt. Repeat with the remaining pretzels. (The baking soda bath is what gives the pretzels that dark brown color—without it, they would be white and doughy.)

7. Bake the pretzels for 12–15 minutes, until they are dark and golden. Let cool for 10 minutes before serving. Enjoy plain, with melted vegan butter, with mustard, or however you enjoy your pretzels.

>>> **Make Ahead** Allow the pretzels to cool completely, then keep in an airtight container at room temperature for up to 3 days. You can reheat by popping in the microwave for a few seconds. You can also freeze the pretzels in an airtight container for up to 6 months.

Sweet & Sour Rice Balls

Have some leftover rice? These rice balls are the perfect way to use it up! These delectable, sticky, slightly crispy little balls make for a fun snack, side dish, or appetizer and are so tasty, you'll never throw out leftover rice again!

MAKES: ABOUT 14 BALLS (4 SERVINGS)	PREP TIME: 10 MINUTES	COOK TIME: 12 MINUTES	TOTAL TIME: 22 MINUTES

FOR THE RICE BALLS

2 cups (500 mL) cooked rice (white rice holds together best)

¼ cup (60 mL) water, plus more if needed

1 tsp white sugar

½ tsp onion powder

¼ tsp garlic powder

¼ tsp salt

FOR THE SAUCE

¼ cup (60 mL) soy sauce (gluten-free if preferred)

2 Tbsp (30 mL) brown sugar

2 Tbsp (30 mL) water

1 Tbsp (15 mL) lime juice

2 tsp cornstarch

2 cloves garlic, minced

FOR ASSEMBLY

Oil, for frying

2 green onions, chopped

1 Tbsp (15 mL) sesame seeds

Crushed red pepper flakes

1. Make the rice balls: In a food processor, combine the rice, water, sugar, onion powder, garlic powder, and salt. Blend, stopping to scrape the sides as needed, until it is smooth and you reach a mashed potato–like consistency. If your rice mixture is too dry, add a bit more water as needed.

2. Take about 2 Tbsp (30 mL) of the rice dough and roll into a small ball. Repeat with remaining dough; you should have about 14 balls.

3. Make the sauce: In a large glass measuring cup or small bowl, whisk together the soy sauce, brown sugar, water, lime juice, cornstarch, and garlic.

4. Cook and assemble the rice balls: Heat about 1 Tbsp (15 mL) oil in a nonstick pan over medium-high heat. Add the rice balls and cook until browned on the bottom. Turn the balls and continue to cook until they are golden on all sides, 5–10 minutes. Pour in the sauce and let cook for 1–2 minutes, until the sauce thickens. Garnish with green onions, sesame seeds, and a pinch of crushed red pepper flakes if desired.

>>> **Make Ahead** Once the rice balls are cool, store in an airtight container in the fridge for up to 3 days. To freeze them, prepare the rice balls following steps 1–2. Spread the balls out on a parchment-lined baking sheet and freeze overnight. Transfer to an airtight container and freeze for up to 3 months. Allow to thaw completely before frying and saucing them.

Stuffed Pasta Shells

This classic Italian dish is now veganized! Large pasta shells are stuffed with tofu ricotta and sautéed spinach and baked in a bed of tomato sauce. This is one of my husband's favorite meals, as it is the perfect combo of carby comfort food and Italian-inspired elegance. Pair this with a simple salad and a nice glass of wine for a special dinner.

SERVES: 6	PREP TIME: 15 MINUTES	COOK TIME: 45 MINUTES	TOTAL TIME: 1 HOUR

14–18 jumbo pasta shells (gluten-free if preferred)

1 Tbsp (15 mL) olive oil

4 cloves garlic, minced

7 oz (200 g) baby spinach

1 recipe Super Quick Tofu Ricotta (page 106)

¼–½ cup (60–125 mL) plant-based milk (such as oat or soy)

1 tsp Italian seasoning

½ tsp salt

½ tsp black pepper

1 jar (22 fl oz/650 mL) prepared tomato sauce or 1 batch Simple Tomato Sauce (page 165)

Fresh basil, chopped, for garnish

1. Preheat your oven to 375°F (190°C).

2. Bring a large pot of water to a boil and cook the pasta according to the package directions. I like to toss in a few extra shells just in case any break while cooking.

3. Heat the oil in a large pan over medium-high heat. Add the garlic and sauté for about 30 seconds, then add the spinach, cover, and reduce the heat to low. Cook the spinach, stirring as needed, until it is wilted, 2–5 minutes.

4. Remove the pan from the heat, then stir in the prepared ricotta, ¼ cup (60 mL) plant-based milk, Italian seasoning, salt, and pepper. If the ricotta mixture is too thick, add more plant-based milk as needed until you reach a thick, creamy consistency.

5. Spread half of the tomato sauce in the bottom of an 8 × 12-inch (20 × 30 cm) baking dish. Stuff each pasta shell with a generous dollop of the spinach ricotta mixture and place in the baking dish. Once all the shells are stuffed, drizzle with the remaining tomato sauce.

6. Cover with foil and bake for 25 minutes. Remove the foil and continue to bake for another 5–10 minutes, until the tomato sauce is bubbling around the edges. Serve hot, garnished with fresh basil.

>>> **Make Ahead** If you wish to prep this ahead of time and then bake it fresh, you can do that. Assemble the stuffed pasta shells and sauce in the baking dish. Cover with plastic wrap or an airtight lid and store in the fridge overnight. Bake when ready to serve. Store leftovers in the fridge for up to 3 days.

Garlic Herb Potato Wedges

These potato wedges are crispy on the outside and pillowy-tender on the inside. Seasoned with a ton of garlic and herbs, these wedges are so tasty that they don't even need a dip! (Although you can totally dip them if you prefer.) You could serve these with my Crunchy Tahini Slaw (page 159) or Four Heads of Garlic Soup (page 123), or you can do as I do and just eat them alone as a meal—carby cravings satisfied!

SERVES: 4	PREP TIME: 10 MINUTES	COOK TIME: 45 MINUTES	TOTAL TIME: 55 MINUTES

3 Tbsp (45 mL) olive oil

6 cloves garlic, minced or pressed

1 tsp salt

1 tsp paprika

½ tsp onion powder

¼ tsp black pepper

4 large russet potatoes, scrubbed clean and cut into thick wedges

1 Tbsp (15 mL) minced fresh parsley

1 Tbsp (15 mL) minced fresh rosemary

1. Preheat your oven to 400°F (200°C) and grab yourself a large baking sheet (no need to grease it).

2. In a glass measuring cup or bowl, mix together the olive oil, garlic, salt, paprika, onion powder, and pepper.

3. Spread the potato wedges across the baking sheet, then drizzle with the olive oil mixture. Toss the wedges to evenly coat them, then ensure they're spread in a single layer so that they aren't overlapping on the baking sheet.

4. Bake for 35–45 minutes, flipping halfway through, until golden all over and tender all the way through when pierced with a fork. Remove from the oven and sprinkle with the parsley and rosemary. Enjoy!

>>> **Make Ahead** I always think wedges are best enjoyed fresh, but if you have leftovers, allow them to cool and then store them in an airtight container in the fridge for up to 4 days.

Double-Potato Cheesy Gnocchi

Pillowy gnocchi are baked in my quick homemade tomato sauce and topped with ooey gooey bubbling potato cheesiness. This dish is quick to throw together but is super impressive in presentation and flavor! Gnocchi is made with potato, so I love pairing this dish with my Creamy Potato Cheese Sauce (page 112) for double the potato fun.

SERVES: 4–6	PREP TIME: 5 MINUTES	COOK TIME: 30 MINUTES	TOTAL TIME: 35 MINUTES

FOR THE TOMATO SAUCE

1 Tbsp (15 mL) olive oil

1 yellow onion, chopped

4 cloves garlic, minced or pressed

1½ cups (375 mL) water

1 can (13 oz/369 g) tomato paste

½ tsp salt

½ tsp crushed red pepper flakes (optional)

FOR THE GNOCCHI

1 package (1 lb/454 g) prepared gnocchi (check to make sure it's vegan) (gluten-free if preferred)

1 bunch fresh basil leaves, removed from stem (set aside some for garnish)

1 batch Creamy Potato Cheese Sauce (page 112)

1. Preheat your oven to 400°F (200°C).

2. Make the tomato sauce: In a large oven-safe skillet or pan, heat the olive oil over medium-high heat. Add the onions and garlic and sauté until the onions turn translucent and begin to brown, about 5 minutes, stirring occasionally. Stir in the water, tomato paste, salt, and red pepper flakes, bring to a simmer, and cook for about 5 minutes.

3. Make the gnocchi: Stir the gnocchi and basil into the sauce and spread it evenly in the pan. Top with dollops of the prepared potato cheese sauce (do not stir it in). Bake until heated through and bubbly, 15–20 minutes. Optionally, turn your broiler on and broil for 30–60 seconds to brown the cheese—keep a close eye on it to ensure it doesn't burn. Remove from the oven, garnish with the remaining basil, and enjoy!

>>> Make Ahead This dish is best served fresh, but leftovers are wonderful as well. Allow to cool before covering and storing in the fridge for up to 3 days.

Cheater Risotto!

If you've been following me for a while, you will know that I love a good hack! Traditionally, making risotto is a very time-consuming process that requires constant attention. Instead of fussing about like that, this is my way to make risotto easily. Just add everything to a Dutch oven or a large oven-safe pot and bake. That's it! Sure, this risotto isn't authentic, but for the time and energy it saves, it's a winner in my opinion! You can enjoy this creamy risotto as is, or you can try one of the delicious add-in options.

SERVES: 6	PREP TIME: 10 MINUTES	COOK TIME: 45 MINUTES	TOTAL TIME: 55 MINUTES

1½ cups (375 mL) arborio rice

5 cups (1.25 L) vegetable broth, warmed, divided

½ cup (125 mL) dry white wine (or sub vegetable broth if preferred)

5 Tbsp (75 mL) nutritional yeast

3 Tbsp (45 mL) vegan butter, diced

¼ tsp salt

½ tsp black pepper

Sunflower Parmesan (page 107), for garnish

OPTIONAL ADD-INS (CHOOSE 1)

PEAS & LEMON

1 cup (250 mL) frozen peas

Zest of 1 lemon

Coarsely ground black pepper

MUSHROOM BACON

2 Tbsp (30 mL) vegan butter

8 oz (227 g) cremini mushrooms or other types of mushrooms

1 Tbsp (15 mL) soy sauce (gluten-free if preferred)

½ Tbsp maple syrup

½ tsp liquid smoke

PAN-ROASTED CHERRY TOMATOES & RICOTTA

1 Tbsp (15 mL) olive oil

1½ cups (375 mL) cherry tomatoes, halved

2 cloves garlic, minced

¼ tsp salt

¼ tsp black pepper

1½ cups (375 mL) Super Quick Tofu Ricotta (page 106)

1. Preheat your oven to 350°F (175°C).

2. in a Dutch oven or large oven-safe pot with a lid, combine the rice and 4 cups (1 L) vegetable broth. Bake for 30–45 minutes, until the rice absorbs most of the broth and is al dente.

3. Carefully remove from the oven and add the wine, nutritional yeast, vegan butter, salt, and pepper (and the peas and lemon zest if you're making that version; see below). Add more vegetable broth to loosen the risotto to the desired consistency (I often use the entire extra cup). Stir the rice vigorously to make it creamy. Serve plain with a sprinkle of sunflower parmesan or with any of the desired add-ins.

Optional Add-Ins

Peas & Lemon: Stir the peas and half of the lemon zest into the hot risotto along with the wine and the remaining ingredients so that the peas heat through. Garnish with the remaining lemon zest and coarsely ground black pepper.

Mushroom Bacon: Melt the vegan butter in a large skillet over medium-high heat. Add the mushrooms, soy sauce, maple syrup, and liquid smoke. Fry the mushrooms for 5–10 minutes, until golden brown and tender.

Try not to stir the mushrooms too much, as letting them rest will allow them to get nice and caramelized. Top the prepared risotto with a spoonful of the mushrooms.

Pan-Roasted Cherry Tomatoes & Ricotta: Heat the oil in a nonstick skillet. When hot, add the cherry tomatoes and cook until they begin to wrinkle a bit, about 2 minutes. They may stick to the pan, so I like to just let them sit without stirring too much. Add the garlic, salt, and pepper and stir, cooking 1–2 minutes more. Spoon over the prepared risotto and top with small spoonfuls of tofu ricotta to taste.

>>> *Make Ahead* Allow the risotto and toppings to cool, then store in separate airtight containers in the fridge for up to 4 days.

Peas & Lemon Risotto

Mushroom Bacon Risotto

Pan-Roasted Cherry
Tomatoes & Ricotta Risotto

Quick Corn Fritters

These corn fritters are quick to whip up and oh so tasty! With buttery, sweet corn and spicy jalapeño, they are lightly crisp on the outside and perfectly chewy on the inside. Yum! I love enjoying these with a little vegan sour cream for dipping. They are also great alongside or on top of a salad for a healthier option, or with a big side of mashed potatoes for a delicious carby meal.

MAKES: ABOUT 10 FRITTERS	PREP TIME: 10 MINUTES	COOK TIME: 25 MINUTES	TOTAL TIME: 35 MINUTES

¾ cup (185 mL) all-purpose flour

¼ cup (60 mL) yellow cornmeal

½ tsp baking powder

¾ tsp salt

¼ tsp black pepper

2 cups (500 mL) frozen corn kernels, thawed and drained

2 cloves garlic, minced

½ yellow onion, finely chopped

½ red bell pepper, finely chopped

½–1 jalapeño, finely minced

½ cup (125 mL) plant-based milk (such as oat or soy)

1–3 Tbsp (15–45 mL) light oil (such as vegetable or canola)

1. In a large bowl, whisk together the flour, cornmeal, baking powder, salt, and pepper. Add the corn, garlic, onions, bell peppers, jalapeños, and plant-based milk and stir well to combine.

2. Heat 1 Tbsp (15 mL) oil in large skillet or nonstick frying pan over medium heat. Use a ⅓-cup (80 mL) measure to scoop the corn batter into the pan, and use the bottom of the measuring cup to flatten the batter out into a circular shape. Repeat, filling the pan with several fritters and keeping them spaced out so they have room to cook—you will need to work in batches, adding more oil to the pan if needed. Fry for 3–4 minutes on one side, until golden and brown. Flip and cook for another 3–4 minutes, until the other side is golden brown and the fritters are cooked through. Transfer to a paper towel–lined plate to drain. Repeat, using up all of the corn batter to make about 10 fritters. Serve hot on their own or with any dips or hot sauce that you like.

>>> **Make Ahead** Allow the fritters to cool, then store in an airtight container in the fridge for up to 4 days or in the freezer for up to 3 months. To reheat the fritters, allow them to thaw first, then warm in the oven at 375°F (190°C) for 10–15 minutes, until heated through.

Carb Lovers' Pizza

CRAVINGS: CARBY, CREAMY
GLUTEN-FREE, MAKE AHEAD, FREEZER-FRIENDLY

Carbs on carbs? Yes, please! Potato pizza is a classic Italian dish. I make mine a little differently by first roasting the potatoes with rosemary and garlic, making them a little crispy, and then drizzling the whole pizza with a creamy white sauce.

MAKES: 1 LARGE PIZZA OR 2 MEDIUM PIZZAS	**PREP TIME:** 20 MINUTES	**COOK TIME:** 45 MINUTES	**TOTAL TIME:** 65 MINUTES

FOR THE PIZZA

- 1½ lb (680 g) Yukon gold or russet potatoes, scrubbed clean and ½-inch (1.2 cm) diced
- 3 Tbsp (45 mL) minced fresh rosemary, divided
- 4 cloves garlic, minced
- 2 Tbsp (30 mL) olive oil, divided
- ½ tsp salt
- ½ tsp black pepper
- 1 batch Cheesy Pizza Dough (page 75), or 22 oz (630 g) store-bought (gluten-free if preferred)
- Pinch of crushed red pepper flakes (optional for spice)

FOR THE WHITE SAUCE

- 1 cup (250 mL) raw cashews, softened if needed
- ½–¾ cup (125–185 mL) water
- 1 Tbsp (15 mL) nutritional yeast
- 1 clove garlic
- ½ tsp salt
- ¼ tsp black pepper

1. Preheat your oven to 450°F (230°C). Lightly grease 1 or 2 pizza pans or baking sheets with oil and set aside.

2. Spread the potatoes over a separate large baking sheet and sprinkle them with 2 Tbsp (30 mL) rosemary, the garlic, 1 Tbsp (15 mL) olive oil, salt, and pepper. Toss well to evenly coat. Bake for about 20 minutes, flipping halfway through, until the potatoes are cooked through and lightly browned (they will crisp more when you bake the pizza).

3. In the meantime, make the white sauce. If you have a high-powered blender, you can skip to the next step. If you don't have a high-powered blender, you should boil the cashews first to ensure they are tender enough to blend into a smooth sauce. To do this, place the cashews in a small pot and cover with water. Bring to a boil and cook for about 10 minutes, until the cashews are very tender. Drain and rinse with cold water.

4. Add the cashews, ½ cup (125 mL) water, nutritional yeast, garlic, salt, and pepper in a blender. Blend until smooth and creamy, stopping to scrape down the sides as needed and adding up to ¼ cup (60 mL) more water if needed to thin.

5. Stretch the pizza dough to make one large or two medium pizzas and place on greased baking trays or pizza pans. Brush the dough with the remaining 1 Tbsp (15 mL) olive oil, then evenly top with the potatoes and a sprinkle of crushed red pepper flakes if desired. Bake for about 15 minutes, until golden brown. Drizzle with white sauce to taste and sprinkle with the remaining 1 Tbsp (15 mL) rosemary.

>>> **Make Ahead** Allow the leftover pizza to cool, then wrap and store in the fridge for up to 4 days or in the freezer for up to 2 months. I like to store the cooked potato pizza and white sauce separately for the best results. Enjoy cold or reheat in the oven or in a cast-iron skillet on the stove.

Cheesy Pizza Dough

This cheesy pizza dough is the best thing since sliced bread! I used to be someone who left the pizza crust on my plate, but not anymore. Seasoning the pizza dough is a game changer—it makes every bite of pizza that much more delicious. Use this recipe to make Carb Lovers' Pizza (page 72) or Three-Cheese Pizza (page 97), or top this pizza dough with any of your favorite toppings.

MAKES: DOUGH FOR 1 LARGE PIZZA OR 2 SMALLER PIZZAS	**PREP TIME:** 15 MINUTES (PLUS 1 HOUR RISING TIME)
COOK TIME: 20 MINUTES	**TOTAL TIME:** 35 MINUTES (PLUS 1 HOUR RISING TIME)

1 cup (250 mL) warm water (think bath-water temperature)

1 Tbsp (15 mL) white sugar

2¼ tsp (1 packet) instant yeast

2½ cups (625 mL) all-purpose flour

2 Tbsp (30 mL) nutritional yeast

1 Tbsp (15 mL) olive oil

1½ tsp salt

½ tsp garlic powder

Note

To make this pizza dough extra cheesy, double both the nutritional yeast and garlic powder. To make this a traditional pizza dough without any cheesy taste, omit the nutritional yeast and garlic powder.

1. In a large mixing bowl, mix together the water, sugar, and yeast. Cover the bowl with a clean dish towel and let rest for 5–10 minutes. Once rested, the mixture should be foamy on top. This is how you know your yeast is good to go! (If it isn't foamy, your yeast is likely too old, so you should purchase new yeast and try again.)

2. Mix in the flour, nutritional yeast, olive oil, salt, and garlic powder to make a dough. Lightly flour a clean work surface and knead the dough for about 5 minutes, until the dough bounces back quickly when poked. Alternatively, you could use a stand mixer with a dough hook.

3. Lightly oil a clean large bowl (I usually just clean the bowl I was just using), and place the dough ball in the bowl. Turn the dough ball around in the bowl to coat it with oil. Cover the bowl with a clean dish towel and set aside somewhere warm to rise for about an hour. (Your oven with just the light turned on is a perfect place.)

4. Once the dough has risen and is about double the size, punch the dough down. This dough recipe makes enough for one large pizza or two smaller pizzas, depending on how thick you like your pizza crust. Bake your prepared pizza in a preheated 450°F (230°C) oven for 15–20 minutes until puffed up and golden.

>>> Make Ahead Place the prepared uncooked pizza dough in a sealable plastic bag, pushing all the extra air out. Store in the fridge for up to 2 days or in the freezer for up to 3 months. You may want to divide the dough into two before freezing it, depending on how thick you like your crust.

No-Knead Crusty Bread

No-knead bread recipes have been circling the web for years! They are just *so* easy to make, and the result is outstanding. Just four ingredients are mixed in a bowl and left covered overnight (no kneading required!). Then, the next day, bake the dough in a Dutch oven (again, no kneading!). Once baked, you'll have the most gorgeous, crusty, warm homemade bread. This recipe is so easy that I make it at least once a week in my house. To make this bread even more fun, I've included some of my favorite optional add-ins.

MAKES: 1 CRUSTY LOAF | **PREP TIME:** 5 MINUTES (PLUS OVERNIGHT RESTING TIME) | **COOK TIME:** 50 MINUTES

TOTAL TIME: 55 MINUTES (PLUS OVERNIGHT RESTING TIME)

---

3 cups (750 mL) all-purpose flour

1½ tsp salt

½ tsp active dry yeast or instant yeast

1½ cups (375 mL) warm water (think bath-water temperature)

OPTIONAL ADD-INS (CHOOSE 1–2)

1 Tbsp (15 mL) sugar, agave, or maple syrup

Coarsely ground black pepper

2 tsp dried herbs (such as Italian seasoning, dried basil leaves, or dried oregano leaves)

3 Tbsp (45 mL) nutritional yeast

3 Tbsp (45 mL) chopped fresh herbs (such as rosemary or sage)

1–2 jalapeños, diced

Up to ¾ cup (185 mL) pitted olives, drained well

Up to ¾ cup (185 mL) chopped sun-dried tomatoes, drained well

Up to ¾ cup (185 mL) chopped nuts (such as walnuts, pistachios, or pecans)

Up to ¾ cup (185 mL) dried cranberries or raisins

1. In a large bowl, whisk together the flour, salt, and yeast. Pour in the water and any additional add-ins if using, and stir to make a dough, making sure all the flour is mixed in. Cover the bowl with plastic wrap and let it sit at room temperature for 10–24 hours. The dough will have doubled in size.

2. When ready to bake the bread, place a Dutch oven or a large oven-safe pot with a lid in your oven. Preheat your oven to 450°F (230°C) with the Dutch oven inside. Once the temperature hits 450°F (230°C), continue to heat the Dutch oven for another 15–20 minutes to ensure it is heated through.

3. Place a large piece of parchment paper on your counter. Using a spatula, gently turn out the dough onto the parchment. You want to keep all of the fluffiness in the dough, so be sure not to punch the dough down. If the dough flattens on the parchment, you can use the spatula to pull the sides up a bit into a rounder shape. If using any toppers, gently brush the loaf with a bit of plant-based milk and sprinkle toppers over the loaf.

4. Making sure to wear oven mitts, remove the lid from the Dutch oven, then pick up the bread using the parchment paper edges to do so. Gently lower the parchment paper into the Dutch oven, then place the lid back on. (It's OK if some parchment paper is sticking out.)

RECIPE CONTINUES ⟶

OPTIONAL CRUST ADDITIONS

(CHOOSE 1–3)

Seeds (such as poppy seeds, sesame seeds, flax, or sunflower seeds)

Dehydrated minced garlic

Dehydrated minced onions

Dried herbs (such as Italian seasoning, dried basil leaves, or caraway)

Rolled oats

5. Bake for 30 minutes with the lid on. Remove the lid, then bake for another 15–20 minutes, until the bread is golden brown and crusty. Carefully remove the Dutch oven and allow the bread to cool in the pot for about 10 minutes before removing.

Note

This recipe also works well with whole wheat flour, but note that the bread will be a bit denser. If making a loaf with 1½ cups (375 mL) all-purpose flour and 1½ cups (375 mL) whole wheat flour, you will need to add 2 Tbsp (30 mL) of extra water. If using all whole wheat flour, you will need to add ¼ cup (60 mL) extra water.

Perfect Flaky Pie Crust

This pie crust is flavorful and flaky, and when baked it has the most beautiful golden color! It's perfect for making sweet and savory pies. It's quick and easy to make (especially when using a food processor), requires only four ingredients, and can be made ahead of time and stored in the fridge or freezer!

MAKES: ONE 9-INCH (23 CM) PIE CRUST | **PREP TIME:** 10 MINUTES (PLUS 20 MINUTES CHILLING TIME)

TOTAL TIME: 10 MINUTES (PLUS 20 MINUTES CHILLING TIME)

1½ cups (375 mL) all-purpose flour, plus more for rolling

1 tsp white sugar, plus more for sprinkling

½ cup (125 mL) cold vegan butter, cubed

¼ cup (60 mL) cold plant-based milk (such as oat or soy)

1–2 Tbsp (15–30 mL) aquafaba (the liquid in a can of chickpeas), for brushing (optional)

Make the Dough

1. Food Processor Method: Place the flour and sugar in a food processor and pulse a few times to mix. Scatter the vegan butter over the flour and pulse several more times until the mixture is a crumbly, sandy texture. Pour in the plant-based milk and pulse a few more times until you reach a shaggy dough but there is still some unmixed flour (don't overmix or the dough will become tough). Turn the dough onto a clean work surface and use your hands to gather everything into a ball. Wrap in plastic wrap and chill in the fridge for at least 20 minutes.

Bowl Method: Place the flour and sugar in a large bowl and whisk to combine. Scatter the vegan butter over the flour and use a fork or pastry cutter to cut the butter into the flour until you reach a crumbly, sandy texture. Drizzle with the plant-based milk and use the fork to combine until you reach a shaggy dough but there is still some unmixed flour (don't overmix or the dough will become tough). Turn the dough onto a clean work surface and use your hands to gather everything into a ball. Wrap in plastic wrap and chill in the fridge for at least 20 minutes.

Roll the Dough

2. Spread a clean, smooth dish towel over your work surface and lightly sprinkle flour over it. Unwrap your dough and place it in the center of the floured towel. Roll out the dough until you have a rough circle that is several inches bigger than your 9-inch (23 cm) pie dish to allow room for the sides and edges of the crust.

RECIPE CONTINUES ⟶

Note

1) Keep everything cold: For the flakiest pie crust, it's important to keep your ingredients cold. It's also helpful to chill your tools (bowl, pastry cutter, food processor blade, rolling pin, etc.) in the fridge before you begin. 2) Double pie crust: If making a double pie crust, double this recipe. When rolling the dough, cut the dough ball in half and work with one half at a time. You can use the second half of the dough to make the top layer of a double-crust pie. Before baking, brush the top generously with aquafaba, and optionally you can sprinkle it with sugar. This will ensure a nice golden-brown crust.

3. Use the towel to help you flip the dough into the pie dish. Use a knife to cut off the excess pastry around the edges. If there are any holes, fill them with some of the extra pieces of dough. Pinch the edges to form a pretty crust. Before baking your pie, you can optionally brush the edges with aquafaba, which will help the crust get extra golden in the oven.

Precook your pie crust (optional)

4. Only do this if the recipe requires a fully cooked crust prior to filling it. Preheat your oven to 450°F (230°C). Pierce the crust all over with a fork. Bake the crust for 15 minutes. Reduce the heat to 400°F (200°C) and continue baking until the crust is lightly browned, 1–3 minutes more.

>>> **Make Ahead** If you would like to prep the pie dough ahead of time, prepare the dough as directed in step 1. Wrap tightly in plastic wrap and place in a sealable bag. Store in the fridge for up to 3 days or in the freezer for up to 6 months. Alternatively, you can prepare the pie crust in the pie plate as directed in step 3. Make sure to use a freezer-safe pie plate. Cover the pastry in plastic wrap or place the entire pie plate in a sealable bag. Store in the fridge for up to 3 days or in the freezer for up to 6 months. Thaw completely at room temperature before using.

ESY

>>> "I could go vegan except for cheese." This is probably one of the most common phrases I hear when people are considering veganism. Well, I have brilliant news for you: you can go vegan AND eat cheese. Vegan cheese, of course. Satisfy those melty, stretchy, gooey, tangy cravings with the recipes in this chapter. Trust me when I say that homemade vegan cheeses are the best, so you're in for a treat with this chapter!

Ooey Gooey Fondue-y

CRAVINGS: CARBY, CHEESY, CREAMY
GLUTEN-FREE, MAKE AHEAD, FREEZER-FRIENDLY

Sometimes there is nothing better than a big pot of cheesy gooeyness to satisfy those cheese cravings! Welcome in, fondue. This tangy, gooey deliciousness is the perfect way to satisfy any cheesy craving. I love to keep it traditional by dipping in cubes of toasted bread, but feel free to dip in anything you want smothered in cheesiness: fruit, potatoes, broccoli . . .

SERVES: 4	**PREP TIME:** 5 MINUTES	**COOK TIME:** 5 MINUTES (PLUS SOFTENING TIME, IF NEEDED)

TOTAL TIME: 10 MINUTES (PLUS SOFTENING TIME, IF NEEDED)

½ cup (125 mL) raw cashews

1¼ cups (310 mL) water

½ cup (125 mL) dry white wine

¼ cup (60 mL) nutritional yeast

3 Tbsp (45 mL) tapioca starch (tapioca flour)

2 Tbsp (30 mL) sauerkraut

½ tsp salt

¼ tsp garlic powder

¼ tsp black pepper

FOR SERVING (CHOOSE WHAT YOU LIKE)

Cubed bread, apple slices, pear slices, grapes, roasted potatoes, roasted Brussels sprouts, steamed broccoli florets, or any other favorite fondue dippers

1. If you have a high-powered blender, you can skip to step 2. If you don't have a high-powered blender, you should boil the cashews first to ensure they are tender enough to blend into a smooth sauce. To do this, place the cashews in a small pot and cover with water. Bring to a boil and cook for about 10 minutes, until the cashews are very tender. Drain and rinse with cold water.

2. Place the cashews, water, wine, nutritional yeast, tapioca starch, sauerkraut, salt, garlic powder, and pepper in your blender and blend until completely smooth. At this stage, the sauce will be quite watery.

3. Pour the fondue mixture into a medium saucepan. Cook over medium-high heat, stirring frequently and scraping the bottom of the pan with a spatula, until the fondue thickens, about 5 minutes. If the sauce gets too thick, just add a splash more water to thin it.

4. Serve hot with your favorite fondue dippers.

>>> **Make Ahead** Allow the fondue to cool, then store in an airtight container in the fridge for up to 4 days or in the freezer for up to 4 months.

Walnut Cacio e Pepe

This dish is inspired by a traditional Italian pasta with pecorino cheese and black pepper. Instead of pecorino, I use walnuts, nutritional yeast, and miso paste to get a similar cheesy taste (trust me on this!). You won't believe how simple and satisfying this recipe is. Creamy, nutty, cheesy, and peppery, it whips up in 15 minutes and pairs well with a simple salad or some green veg.

SERVES: 4–6	PREP TIME: 5 MINUTES	COOK TIME: 10 MINUTES	TOTAL TIME: 15 MINUTES

1 lb (454 g) spaghetti (gluten-free if preferred)

1 cup (250 mL) raw walnuts

1 cup (250 mL) water

¼ cup (60 mL) nutritional yeast

2 Tbsp (30 mL) white miso paste

½ tsp salt (or to taste)

1 tsp freshly cracked black pepper (or to taste)

1. Bring a large pot of water to a boil and cook your spaghetti according to the package directions. Before draining, reserve 1 cup (250 mL) of pasta water and set aside.

2. In the meantime, make the sauce by placing the walnuts, water, nutritional yeast, white miso paste, and salt in a blender. Blend until smooth, scraping down the sides of the blender as needed. The sauce will have a slight texture from the walnuts, and this is good! Add the pepper and pulse to combine.

3. Add the cooked and drained spaghetti back to the pot. Pour in the sauce and toss well. If needed, add a splash of the reserved pasta water to loosen the pasta. Garnish with another fresh crack of pepper and serve hot.

>>> Make Ahead Store the sauce in an airtight container in the fridge for up to 3 days, then simply toss with hot pasta, adding reserved cooking water if needed. Leftover pasta can be cooled and stored in an airtight container in the fridge for up to 3 days.

Super Simple Queso

This super creamy, rich, silky cheese sauce can be whipped up in just 5 minutes if you have a high-powered blender, or 15 if you don't. It's fantastic served hot or cold. I love enjoying it in my Crunch Wrap Superior (page 202) or with veggies or tortilla chips for dipping. You can also drizzle this over steamed cauliflower or broccoli, spoon it onto a baked potato, or even toss it with noodles. Enjoy this yumminess everywhere!

MAKES: ABOUT 2 CUPS (500 ML)	PREP TIME: 5 MINUTES	COOK TIME: 10 MINUTES (IF NEEDED)	TOTAL TIME: 5–15 MINUTES

1 cup (250 mL) raw cashews (see note)

¾ cup (185 mL) plant-based milk (such as oat or soy)

¼ cup (60 mL) nutritional yeast

1 tsp taco seasoning

½ tsp salt

Note

Raw cashews are my favorite because they get the creamiest, but if you need an alternative, try subbing them with blanched almonds, macadamia nuts, or raw sunflower seeds. If using one of these nut or seed options, boil them for 15 minutes before using to ensure that they are softened and will blend smoothly.

1. If you do not have a high-powered blender, you will first need to boil the cashews to ensure they blend smoothly. To do so, cover the cashews with water in a medium pot and bring to a boil. Cook for about 10 minutes, until the cashews are very tender. Drain and rinse with cold water before using.

2. Place the raw or boiled cashews in a blender along with the plant-based milk, nutritional yeast, taco seasoning, and salt. Blend until smooth and creamy. Enjoy cold, or heat in the microwave or in a small pot on the stove if desired.

>>> Make Ahead Store in an airtight container in the fridge for up to 4 days or in the freezer for up to 4 months.

Beer & Cheese Soup

All the pubs in the world should serve up this cheesy beer-infused soup! The creamy cheesiness comes from my favorite nut friend: raw cashews. When the cashews are simmered in the soup, they become tender and easy to blend with the rest of the ingredients. The result? Rich, flavor-packed, lightly spicy, cheesy perfection in a bowl.

SERVES: 4–6	PREP TIME: 15 MINUTES	COOK TIME: 15 MINUTES	TOTAL TIME: 30 MINUTES

FOR THE SOUP

- 2 Tbsp (30 mL) vegan butter
- 2 medium carrots, peeled and chopped
- 2 ribs celery, chopped
- 1 yellow onion, chopped
- 1 jalapeño, chopped
- 4 cloves garlic, minced or pressed
- ¼ cup (60 mL) all-purpose flour (gluten-free if preferred)
- 1 can (16 fl oz/500 mL) light lager (gluten-free if preferred, see note)
- 3 cups (750 mL) vegetable broth
- ½ cup (125 mL) raw cashews (see note)
- ¼ cup (60 mL) nutritional yeast
- 1 tsp smoked paprika
- 1 tsp dried thyme leaves or 1 Tbsp (15 mL) fresh
- ½ tsp salt
- ¼ tsp black pepper

FOR THE CROUTONS

- 1 Tbsp (15 mL) vegan butter
- 2 slices bread, chopped into 1-inch (2.5 cm) cubes (gluten-free if preferred)
- 1 Tbsp (15 mL) nutritional yeast
- ½ tsp smoked paprika
- ¼ tsp salt

FOR GARNISH

- 1 jalapeño, thinly sliced
- A few pinches of fresh thyme leaves

1. Make the soup: In a large soup pot, melt the vegan butter over medium-high heat. Add the carrots, celery, onions, chopped jalapeños, and garlic and sauté until the veggies have softened and begin to brown, about 5 minutes. Sprinkle the flour over the vegetables and stir, cooking the flour for about 1 minute more. Add the lager, broth, cashews, nutritional yeast, smoked paprika, thyme, salt, and pepper. Bring to a simmer and cook for about 10 minutes, until the cashews have softened.

2. Carefully transfer the soup to your blender (you may need to work in batches) and blend until completely smooth and creamy. Be careful not to overfill the blender so that the soup doesn't erupt. Return the soup to the pot to keep warm over low heat. (Alternatively, an immersion blender will work in a pinch, but I generally prefer a standing blender as it usually does a better job of blending the cashews into a smooth cream.)

3. Make the croutons: Melt the vegan butter in a skillet or frying pan over medium-high heat. Add the bread cubes, nutritional yeast, smoked paprika, and salt. Stir to coat evenly, and cook until the bread cubes have turned golden brown and are crispy. Serve the soup hot with croutons, jalapeño slices, and thyme for garnish.

>>> **Make Ahead** Allow the soup to cool, then store in an airtight container in the fridge for up to 4 days. Store the croutons separately in an airtight container at room temperature for up to 4 days. You can also freeze both separately in airtight containers. The soup can be kept frozen for up to 3 months, and the croutons for up to 6 weeks.

Note

1) If you aren't a fan of beer, sub it with
2 extra cups (500 mL) vegetable broth.

2) You can sub raw cashews with
macadamia nuts, blanched almonds,
or raw sunflower seeds.

Baked Panko Mac & Cheese

CRAVINGS: CARBY, CHEESY, CREAMY, CRUNCHY
GLUTEN-FREE, MAKE AHEAD

Is there anything more satisfying than creamy macaroni topped with a golden, crispy panko topping? This mac and cheese is easy to whip up and feeds a crowd that will soon be very satisfied!

SERVES: 8	PREP TIME: 5 MINUTES	COOK TIME: 45 MINUTES (PLUS SOFTENING TIME, IF NEEDED)

TOTAL TIME: 50 MINUTES (PLUS SOFTENING TIME, IF NEEDED)

1 lb (454 g) (3 cups/750 mL) elbow macaroni (gluten-free if preferred)

FOR THE CHEESE SAUCE
1 cup (250 mL) raw cashews

3½ cups (875 mL) water

⅓ cup (80 mL) nutritional yeast

¼ cup (60 mL) cornstarch

2 Tbsp (30 mL) white miso paste

2 Tbsp (30 mL) lemon juice

2 tsp paprika

1 tsp salt

½ tsp garlic powder

¼ tsp turmeric

¼ tsp black pepper

FOR THE PANKO TOPPING
1½ cups (375 mL) panko breadcrumbs (gluten-free if preferred)

¼ cup (60 mL) vegan butter, melted

¼ cup (60 mL) nutritional yeast

¼ tsp paprika

1. If you have a high-powered blender, you can skip to step 2. If you don't have a high-powered blender, you should boil the cashews first to ensure they are tender enough to blend into a smooth sauce. To do this, place the cashews in a small pot and cover with water. Bring to a boil and cook for about 10 minutes, until the cashews are very tender. Drain and rinse with cold water. Alternatively, you can let them soak in water overnight instead of boiling.

2. Preheat your oven to 350°F (175°C). Lightly grease a 9 × 13-inch (23 × 33 cm) baking dish.

3. Bring a large pot of water to a boil and cook the macaroni according to the package directions, until it is about 1 minute away from al dente (it will finish cooking in the oven). Drain and set aside.

4. Make the cheese sauce: Place the cashews, water, nutritional yeast, cornstarch, miso paste, lemon juice, paprika, salt, garlic powder, turmeric, and pepper in your blender. Blend until completely smooth (it will be very watery), stopping to scrape the sides as needed.

5. Return the pot to the stove *without* the pasta in it, and pour in the cheese sauce. Cook over medium-high heat, stirring often. It will begin to form lumps and thicken. Once thickened, about 5 minutes, add the pasta back to the pot and stir to mix it into the sauce. Pour the mac and cheese into the prepared baking dish and spread evenly.

6. Make the panko topping: In a small bowl, combine the panko, melted vegan butter, nutritional yeast, and paprika.

7. Sprinkle the panko topping over the macaroni. Bake, uncovered, until golden on top, 25–30 minutes. Serve hot.

>>> *Make Ahead* Allow the leftovers to cool, then cover and store in the fridge for up to 3 days.

Note

If needed, you can replace cashews with macadamia nuts, blanched almonds, or raw sunflower seeds. If using one of these options, boil them for 15 minutes before using to ensure that they are softened and blend smoothly.

My Favorite Snacking Cheese

When I have cheesy cravings, sometimes I just want good ol' cheese and crackers. These days, we are lucky that many stores carry fancy vegan cheeses, but they can be very pricey, and not always very tasty, so I love making my own quick homemade versions! They are not only easy to make, but you can control the taste. This cheese is cheddary, slightly smoky, and perfectly spreadable.

MAKES: 2 WHEELS OF CHEESE (ABOUT 4 INCHES/10 CM IN DIAMETER)	**PREP TIME:** 15 MINUTES (PLUS CHILLING TIME)
COOK TIME: 10 MINUTES (PLUS SOFTENING TIME)	**TOTAL TIME:** 25 MINUTES (PLUS CHILLING AND SOFTENING TIME)

2 cups (500 mL) raw cashews (see note)

¼ cup (60 mL) nutritional yeast

5 Tbsp (75 mL) refined coconut oil, melted (see note)

2 Tbsp (30 mL) lemon juice

2 Tbsp (30 mL) white miso paste

1 tsp onion powder

1 tsp smoked paprika

¾ tsp salt (or to taste)

¼ tsp turmeric

¼ tsp black pepper

Crackers, grapes, olives, cornichons, or other cheeseboard favorites, for serving

>>> **Make Ahead** I love making this recipe and having it ready to enjoy! Wrap the finished cheese in plastic wrap, wax paper, parchment paper, or wax wrap, then place in a sealable bag or airtight container. Store in the fridge for up to 2 weeks or in the freezer for up to 6 months. You can enjoy it extra-firm straight from the freezer or allow it to thaw in the fridge.

1. You will need to soften your cashews for this recipe to ensure that they can blend smoothly. To soften the cashews, you can either boil or soak them.

Boil the cashews (the fast method): Place the cashews in a small pot, cover with water, and boil for about 10 minutes, until the cashews are very tender. Drain and rinse before using.

Soak the cashews (the slow method): Place the cashews in a bowl and cover with water. Let soak for 4 hours or overnight, until tender. Drain and rinse before using.

2. Line a mold or dish with plastic wrap or cheesecloth—you can use any shaped dish or mold you like; I used two 4-inch (10 cm) mini springform pans to make two wheels of cheese.

3. Place the softened cashews, nutritional yeast, coconut oil, lemon juice, miso paste, onion powder, smoked paprika, salt, turmeric, and pepper in your food processor and blend to make it as smooth as possible, stopping to scrape the sides as needed. The cheese will become warm and sticky, and this is when you know you've reached the right amount of blending.

4. Scoop the cheese into the prepared mold(s). Cover and chill in the fridge for 6 hours or overnight. The cheese will set better the longer you chill it. To make the cheese extra-firm, you can pop it in the freezer for 30 minutes before serving. Serve with crackers, grapes, olives, cornichons, or other cheeseboard favorites.

Note

1) Coconut oil is what makes this cheese get firm. You can try substituting vegetable shortening if needed. You can also omit the oil, but this will mean the cheese will not firm up and will stay a softer texture.

2) You can sub raw cashews with macadamia nuts, blanched almonds, or raw sunflower seeds. You'll need to boil the almonds and raw sunflower seeds for closer to 15 minutes to ensure they are soft and blendable.

Three-Cheese Pizza

Cheesy pizza dough is spread with creamy alfredo sauce and then topped with cheddary coconut cheese. Oh yes, this is real, and you can make this happen in your very own kitchen. Then you will thank me and make this a regular repeat, because vegan cheese pizza is EVERYTHING!

MAKES: 1 LARGE PIZZA OR 2 MEDIUM PIZZAS	**PREP TIME:** 10 MINUTES	**COOK TIME:** 25 MINUTES	**TOTAL TIME:** 35 MINUTES

1 batch Cheesy Pizza Dough (page 75, see note) (or use store-bought gluten-free pizza dough if preferred)

1 batch Cheddary Coconut Cheese Sauce (page 111)

FOR THE ALFREDO SAUCE

¼ cup (60 mL) vegan butter

8 cloves garlic, minced or pressed

¼ cup (60 mL) all-purpose flour (gluten-free if preferred)

2 cups (500 mL) plant-based milk (such as oat or soy)

1 tsp dried parsley flakes

¼ tsp salt

Note

You can use store-bought pizza dough or a gluten-free pizza crust option if you prefer. Just note that the crust will not taste cheesy.

1. Preheat your oven to 450°F (230°C). Lightly grease one or two pizza baking pans.

2. Make the alfredo sauce: Melt the vegan butter in a medium pan over medium-high heat. Add the garlic and cook for about 1 minute, until it becomes fragrant but doesn't brown. Whisk in the flour to make a paste, then cook, whisking frequently, for another minute. Whisk in the plant-based milk, parsley, and salt. Continue cooking for another few minutes, whisking often, until it thickens into a nice sauce. Remove from the heat.

3. If making one large pizza, stretch the dough so that it fits your pizza pan. If making two pizzas, divide the dough into two and stretch the dough to make two pizzas.

4. Spread the pizza(s) with the alfredo sauce, then swirl the cheddary coconut cheese sauce on top of that. If you are making one pizza, you may have extra cheese and alfredo sauces. Set them aside and use the leftovers for dipping pizza crust into! Bake for 15–20 minutes, keeping a close eye so that the pizza doesn't burn, until the crust is lightly golden and the cheese is bubbly and starting to brown. Remove from the heat and allow to rest for 5 minutes before slicing.

>>> Make Ahead You can prepare the pizza dough, cheddary coconut cheese sauce, and alfredo sauce ahead of time and store them separately in airtight containers in the fridge for up to 3 days. The cheese and alfredo sauces may thicken when chilled, so you may want to gently reheat them in the microwave or in pots on the stove, adding a splash more water to loosen them if needed.

This is the most epic comfort food!

Cheesy Pull-Apart Garlic Bread

CRAVINGS: CARBY, CHEESY
GLUTEN-FREE, MAKE AHEAD, FREEZER-FRIENDLY

Garlic butter, stretchy cashew cheese, crusty bread—what's not to like? This is the most epic comfort food. You can enjoy this as a side along with pizza, pasta, or soup. But personally, I like to enjoy this as an appetizer or a fun snack with a few friends.

SERVES: 6–8	PREP TIME: 15 MINUTES	COOK TIME: 30 MINUTES (PLUS SOFTENING TIME, IF NEEDED)

TOTAL TIME: 45 MINUTES (PLUS SOFTENING TIME, IF NEEDED)

FOR THE STRETCHY CASHEW CHEESE (SEE NOTE)

½ cup (125 mL) raw cashews

1 cup (250 mL) plant-based milk (such as oat or soy)

3 Tbsp (45 mL) tapioca starch (tapioca flour)

2 Tbsp (30 mL) nutritional yeast

2 tsp lemon juice

1 tsp salt

FOR ASSEMBLY

1 loaf No-Knead Crusty Bread (page 77) or store-bought crusty bread (gluten-free if preferred, see note)

¼ cup (60 mL) vegan butter

2 cloves garlic, minced or pressed

1 Tbsp (15 mL) chopped fresh parsley

Make the Stretchy Cashew Cheese

1. If you do not have a high-powered blender, you will need to soften the cashews to make sure they blend smoothly. To soften the cashews, you can either boil or soak them.

Boil the cashews (the fast method): Place the cashews in a small pot, cover with water, and boil for about 10 minutes, until the cashews are very tender. Drain and rinse before using.

Soak the cashews (the slow method): Place the cashews in a bowl and cover with water. Let soak for 4 hours or overnight, until tender. Drain and rinse before using.

2. Place the cashews, plant-based milk, tapioca starch, nutritional yeast, lemon juice, and salt in your blender. Blend until completely smooth and creamy. If you do not have a high-powered blender, I also recommend straining the cheese sauce before cooking it, to remove any little cashew bits so the cheese will be smooth.

3. Pour the sauce into a medium saucepan and set over medium-high heat. Stir often while it cooks. The cheese sauce will begin to form lumps, and then come together into a sticky cheesy sauce in about 5 minutes. Remove from the heat.

RECIPE CONTINUES ⟶

Assemble the Pull-Apart Bread

4. Preheat your oven to 350°F (175°C).

5. Cut your loaf in a crosshatch pattern, making slices every inch in both directions, cutting most of the way through, and leaving the bottom intact so that it doesn't fall apart.

6. In a small bowl, whip together the vegan butter, garlic, and parsley. Spread between the bread cuts.

7. Take small spoonfuls of the cashew cheese and squish them between the bread cuts. Repeat, using up all the cheese to fill the bread.

8. Wrap the prepared bread loaf with aluminum foil and bake for 15 minutes. Unwrap the foil and bake another 5–10 minutes, until the cheese is gooey and the bread is lightly golden brown. Serve hot.

>>> **Make Ahead** If prepping ahead, prepare the loaf of bread with the garlic butter and stuff it with cheese (steps 1–7). Wrap in foil and store in the fridge for up to 2 days, or wrap it well, place in a freezer bag, and freeze for up to 4 months. Allow to thaw and come to room temperature. Bake when ready to enjoy.

Potachos

It's potatoes, it's nachos, it's potachos!! Thin slices of potato are topped with creamy red pepper cheese sauce, chewy tofu crumbles, and any of your favorite nacho fixings. This is one of my favorite comfort foods to enjoy with some excellently bad reality TV! And because it's made with potatoes and homemade cheese, it's actually pretty healthy for you too. Bonus points!

SERVES: 2–4	**PREP TIME:** 30 MINUTES	**COOK TIME:** 1 HOUR 5 MINUTES	**TOTAL TIME:** 1 HOUR 35 MINUTES

FOR THE TOFU CRUMBLES

2 Tbsp (30 mL) soy sauce (gluten-free if preferred)

1 Tbsp (15 mL) olive oil

1 tsp chili powder

1 tsp garlic powder

1 tsp onion powder

1 tsp smoked paprika

1 block (12 oz/340 g) extra-firm tofu, drained

FOR THE POTATOES

2 lb (907 g) skin-on russet potatoes, cut into ¼-inch (6 mm) slices

Cooking spray

½ tsp salt

Roasted Red Pepper Cheese Sauce (page 114, see note)

FOR THE TOPPINGS (CHOOSE AS MANY AS YOU LIKE)

Vegan sour cream

Black beans

Fresh cilantro, coarsely chopped

Jalapeño, thinly sliced

Tomato, diced

Salsa

Guacamole

Avocado, chopped

1. Make the tofu crumbles: Preheat your oven to 350°F (175°C). Line a large baking sheet with parchment paper or lightly grease it.

2. In a large bowl, mix together the soy sauce, oil, chili powder, garlic powder, onion powder, and smoked paprika. Using your fingers, crumble the block of tofu into the bowl with the seasoning, or use a potato masher to smash the tofu into crumbles. Mix the tofu crumbles with the seasoning, making sure that all of the tofu is evenly coated.

3. Spread the tofu crumbles evenly over the prepared pan. Bake for 25–30 minutes, stopping to stir the tofu every now and then, until lightly browned. Remove the tofu from the oven and turn the oven up to 450°F (230°C).

4. Make the potatoes: Fill a large bowl with cold water and soak the potato slices in the water for 20 minutes. (Soaking the potatoes helps them get crispy.) Drain the potatoes and pat them dry with a clean dish towel.

5. Lightly grease two large baking sheets. Arrange the potato slices in a single layer on each baking sheet—don't overlap them. Spray the potato slices with the cooking spray, then sprinkle with salt. Bake for 15 minutes, flip the potatoes, and bake for another 10–15 minutes, until browned on both sides. While they are cooking, keep a close eye on them and remove any potatoes that are starting to burn from the pan; you can add them back in later.

RECIPE CONTINUES ⟶

Note

I love my Roasted Red Pepper Cheese Sauce (page 114) for this dish because it adds so much flavor, but feel free to also try the Creamy Potato Cheese Sauce (page 112), Cheddary Coconut Cheese Sauce (page 111), or store-bought vegan cheese shreds.

6. When the potatoes are cooked, pile all of the potato slices on one baking sheet or in another heatproof dish. Drizzle the red pepper cheese sauce on top and sprinkle with the tofu crumbles. Return to the oven for 3–5 minutes to heat through. Remove from the oven and garnish with your favorite optional toppings. Serve right away.

>>> **Make Ahead** You can make the tofu crumbles and the cheese sauce ahead of time and store them in separate airtight containers in the fridge for up to 4 days or in the freezer for up to 3 months. You can also slice the potatoes ahead of time and allow them to soak in the water in the fridge for 20 minutes or up to overnight.

White Lasagna

This white lasagna tastes like sinful cheesy, dreamy comfort food, but is disguised as a fancy dinner. Yes! With four layers of noodles, a quick homemade tofu ricotta, and a creamy spinach sauce, this lasagna is a crowd-pleaser!

SERVES: 9	PREP TIME: 15 MINUTES	COOK TIME: 45 MINUTES	TOTAL TIME: 1 HOUR

12 lasagna noodles (gluten-free if preferred)

FOR THE CREAMY SPINACH SAUCE

½ cup (125 mL) vegan butter, divided

2 medium yellow onions (or 1 large), thinly sliced

6 cloves garlic, minced or pressed

½ cup (125 mL) all-purpose flour (gluten-free if preferred)

4 cups (1 L) plant-based milk (such as oat or soy, see note)

¼ cup (60 mL) nutritional yeast

1 tsp salt

11 oz (312 g) baby spinach

FOR ASSEMBLY

1 batch Super Quick Tofu Ricotta (page 106)

Sunflower Parmesan (optional, page 107)

Note

Ensure you use an unsweetened plant-based milk that is neutral in flavor, but also one that you really enjoy the taste of. Since you use so much plant-based milk in this recipe, you can really taste it—so make sure it's a favorite!

1. Preheat your oven to 400°F (200°C). Lightly grease a 9 × 13-inch (23 × 33 cm) baking dish.

2. Cook the lasagna noodles according to the package directions and set aside.

3. Make the creamy spinach sauce: Melt the vegan butter in a large pot over medium-high heat. Add the onions and garlic and sauté until the onions turn translucent and begin to brown, 5–8 minutes, stirring occasionally. Sprinkle in the flour and stir it into the onions. Cook, stirring frequently, for about 1 minute. Mix in the plant-based milk, nutritional yeast, and salt. Bring to a simmer and gently cook, stirring often, until the sauce thickens, about 10 minutes. Stir in the spinach and let it wilt into the sauce. Remove from the heat. You are now ready to assemble the lasagna.

4. Assemble the lasagna: Spread 1 heaping cup (250 mL) of the creamy spinach sauce across the bottom of the prepared pan. Top with three lasagna noodles. (If the lasagna noodles are sticking together, simply rinse them with a bit of water to loosen them.) Spread 1 more heaping cup (250 mL) of creamy spinach sauce, and sprinkle over one-third of the ricotta. Top with three more noodles, followed by 1 heaping cup (250 mL) creamy spinach sauce, and another third of the ricotta. Repeat to make the final layer: three noodles, 1 heaping cup (250 mL) creamy spinach sauce, and the remaining third of the ricotta. Top with the last three noodles and the remaining spinach sauce.

5. Bake for 25 minutes, until heated through and bubbling. Optionally, to finish, you can brown the top by putting the lasagna under the broiler for 1–2 minutes until it's browned and bubbly. Let rest for 15–20 minutes at room temperature before serving. If you'd like, you can garnish with a sprinkle of sunflower parmesan.

>>> **Make Ahead** You can prepare the lasagna up to the baking step (steps 1–4). Allow to cool, then wrap and store in the fridge for up to 2 days, or freeze for up to 1 month. When you'd like to bake it, preheat your oven to 400°F (200°C) and allow the lasagna to thaw completely and come to room temperature before baking. To bake, follow step 5. This lasagna also makes for great leftovers; once cooled, store it in the fridge for up to 4 days.

Super Quick Tofu Ricotta

CRAVINGS: CHEESY, CREAMY
GLUTEN-FREE, MAKE AHEAD, ONE POT

Easy to make and very versatile, this is a fantastic recipe to have on hand for adding some savory cheesiness to any dish. This is great spread on toast, enjoyed with some crackers, or dolloped onto tomato pizza. In this book, I also use it in my White Lasagna (page 104) and Stuffed Pasta Shells (page 60).

MAKES: ABOUT 1½ CUPS (4–6 SERVINGS)	**PREP TIME:** 5 MINUTES	**TOTAL TIME:** 5 MINUTES

1 block (12 oz/340 g) extra-firm tofu, drained

2 Tbsp (30 mL) lemon juice

2 Tbsp (30 mL) nutritional yeast

2 Tbsp (30 mL) white miso paste

1 tsp onion powder

½ tsp garlic powder

½ tsp salt

1. Place all the ingredients in a food processor and blend until smooth and creamy. If you do not have a food processor, place all the ingredients in a bowl and use a potato masher or immersion blender to mix everything together until it's as smooth as possible.

>>> **Make Ahead** Store in an airtight container in the fridge for up to 1 week.

Sunflower Parmesan

Most vegan parmesan recipes are made using cashews. I love this sunflower seed version because it's not only nut-allergy-friendly, but also much more affordable, and I think it's even more delicious than the cashew version! The secret ingredient in this recipe is lemon pepper. This adds a tanginess to the parmesan, which is to-die-for delicious. If you don't have any lemon pepper on hand, you can try subbing it with an equal amount of dried lemon zest and a sprinkle of black pepper.

MAKES: ABOUT 1¼ CUPS (310 ML)	**PREP TIME:** 5 MINUTES	**TOTAL TIME:** 5 MINUTES

1 cup (250 mL) raw or roasted sunflower seeds

⅓ cup (80 mL) nutritional yeast

1 tsp garlic powder

1 tsp lemon pepper

½ tsp salt

1. Place everything in a blender or food processor and pulse to combine and break down the sunflower seeds into a fine crumble. I like mine with a bit of texture, but if you prefer more of a powder, pulse a few more times. Be careful not to overblend or it will start to turn into sunflower seed butter!

>>> **Make Ahead** Store sunflower parmesan in a sealed jar in the fridge for several weeks or in the freezer for up to 6 months.

Tangy Blue Cheese

CRAVINGS: CHEESY, CREAMY
GLUTEN-FREE, MAKE AHEAD, FREEZER-FRIENDLY

With just eight ingredients, you can make your own homemade vegan blue cheese! This dairy-free cheese is creamy and tangy, has that funky kick to it, and even has the pretty green and blue veins throughout! This cheese is perfect for a vegan charcuterie board, for crumbling onto salad, or for topping a delicious sandwich or The Best Burger Ever (page 224).

MAKES: 2 WHEELS OF CHEESE (ABOUT 4 INCHES/10 CM IN DIAMETER)		**PREP TIME:** 10 MINUTES (PLUS 3 HOURS CHILLING TIME)
COOK TIME: 10 MINUTES	**TOTAL TIME:** 20 MINUTES (PLUS 3 HOURS CHILLING TIME)	

2 cups (500 mL) raw cashews (see note)

¼ cup (60 mL) refined coconut oil, melted (see note)

3 Tbsp (45 mL) apple cider vinegar

3 Tbsp (45 mL) white miso paste

1½ tsp salt

1 tsp onion powder

½ tsp garlic powder

¼ tsp spirulina (for blue-green veins, see note)

Crackers or bread, for serving (optional)

>>> **Make Ahead** Wrap the firmed-up cheese and store in a sealable bag or airtight container in the fridge for up to 2 weeks or in the freezer for up to 6 months. You can enjoy it extra-firm straight from the freezer or allow it to thaw in the fridge.

1. Place the cashews in a medium pot and cover with water. Set over high heat and bring to a boil. Boil for about 10 minutes, until the cashews are tender. Drain and rinse with cold water. Alternatively, you can soak the cashews by placing them in a bowl, covering them with water, and allowing them to soak for a minimum of 6 hours or overnight. Drain and rinse before using. Both of these methods will soften the cashews, making them easier to blend into a creamy texture.

2. Place the softened cashews, coconut oil, apple cider vinegar, miso paste, salt, onion powder, and garlic powder in a food processor. Blend, stopping to scrape the sides as needed, until the mixture becomes as smooth as possible. It will become a bit sticky and will be warm from the friction.

3. Line a mold or dish with plastic wrap or cheesecloth—you can use any shaped dish or mold you like; I used two 4-inch (10 cm) mini springform pans to make two wheels of cheese. Alternatively, you can make one large block of cheese.

4. **Form the cheese:** Scoop about half of the cheese mixture into the mold(s) and spread out. Sprinkle about half of the spirulina across the surface. Add the remaining cheese mixture, and sprinkle with the remaining spirulina. Use a knife to stir the cheese in the mold two to three times to mix in the spirulina and create veins in the cheese. Don't overmix. Smooth the top of the cheese, then cover and chill in the fridge for 6 hours or overnight to let the cheese firm up. The cheese will be firmer fresh out of the fridge but will soften as it sits out. You can also pop it in the freezer for about 30 minutes before serving to make it even firmer. Serve with crackers or bread.

Cheddary Coconut Cheese Sauce

Coconut milk makes this cheddary cheese sauce extra rich and luxurious—and all in just 5 minutes of cooking time! Bea-u-tiful! This super simple cheese is great when used to make cheesy fries, quick grilled cheese sandwiches, and my Three-Cheese Pizza (page 97).

MAKES: ABOUT 2 CUPS (500 ML)	**COOK TIME:** 5 MINUTES	**TOTAL TIME:** 5 MINUTES

1 can (13½ fl oz/400 mL) full-fat coconut milk (see note)

¼ cup (60 mL) nutritional yeast

3 Tbsp (45 mL) tapioca starch (tapioca flour)

1½ tsp paprika

½ tsp onion powder

½ tsp salt

1. Place all the ingredients in a medium saucepan and whisk together well.

2. Set the pan over medium-high heat and cook, stirring often. The mixture will start to form clumps and gradually turn into a thick cheesy sauce, about 5 minutes. Remove from the heat and enjoy!

>>> **Make Ahead** Allow the sauce to cool, then store in an airtight container in the fridge for up to 3 days or in the freezer for up to 4 months.

Note

Coconut milk is high in fat, which is why it's perfect for this recipe, but if you need to substitute it, try using a plant-based culinary cream or another plant-based milk that is extra rich.

Creamy Potato Cheese Sauce

We all know and love mashed potatoes, but have you ever considered how creamy potatoes can be? The texture and mild flavor of potatoes are perfect for making a gorgeous cheesy sauce. Use this recipe in my Double-Potato Cheesy Gnocchi (page 65), drizzle it over nachos, dip veggies into it, or pour it onto roasted veggies. I'm particularly obsessed with pairing this with roasted broccoli! Omnomnom!

MAKES: ABOUT 2 CUPS (500 ML)	**PREP TIME:** 5 MINUTES	**COOK TIME:** 10 MINUTES	**TOTAL TIME:** 15 MINUTES

1 medium russet potato (about 7 oz/200 g), peeled and cubed

¼ cup (60 mL) raw cashews (see note)

½–¾ cup (125–185 mL) plant-based milk (such as oat or soy)

2 Tbsp (30 mL) nutritional yeast

2 Tbsp (30 mL) sauerkraut

½ tsp onion powder

½ tsp salt

¼ tsp garlic powder

1. Place the potatoes and cashews in a medium pot and cover with water. Bring to a boil and cook until the potatoes are fork-tender, 5–10 minutes. Drain and rinse.

2. Place the cooked potatoes and cashews in a blender along with ½ cup (125 mL) plant-based milk, nutritional yeast, sauerkraut, onion powder, salt, and garlic powder and blend until smooth and creamy. If needed, add more plant-based milk, 1 Tbsp (15 mL) at a time, to reach the desired cheesy texture. Enjoy cold, or heat in a small pot or in the microwave.

>>> **Make Ahead** Allow the sauce to cool, then store in an airtight container in the fridge for up to 4 days or in the freezer for up to 4 months.

Note

You can sub cashews with macadamia nuts, blanched almonds, or raw sunflower seeds. To ensure that the nuts or seeds get creamy, you may want to boil them separately for 10 minutes before adding the potatoes and continuing to boil.

Roasted Red Pepper Cheese Sauce

CRAVINGS: CHEESY, CREAMY
GLUTEN-FREE, MAKE AHEAD, FREEZER-FRIENDLY, ONE POT

Roasted red peppers add so much depth of flavor to this cheese sauce—it's perfect for anywhere cheesiness is desired! I love this sauce on my Potachos (page 101) or for dipping bread or veggies.

MAKES: ABOUT 1½ CUPS (375 ML)	**PREP TIME:** 5 MINUTES	**COOK TIME:** 10 MINUTES (IF NEEDED)	**TOTAL TIME:** 5–15 MINUTES

¾ cup (185 mL) raw cashews

½ cup (125 mL) plant-based milk (such as oat or soy)

1 roasted red bell pepper (see page 12) or 1 jar (8 oz/227 g), drained

3 Tbsp (45 mL) nutritional yeast

1 Tbsp (15 mL) lemon juice or apple cider vinegar

½ tsp salt

½ tsp onion powder

¼ tsp garlic powder

Note

1) For convenience, I like to use jarred roasted red peppers. If you prefer, you can roast your own red peppers using the method on page 12.. 2) I love how cashews add so much creaminess to this cheese, but other great substitutes are macadamia nuts, blanched almonds, or raw sunflower seeds. If using these nut or seed options, boil them for 15 minutes to ensure they are softened and will blend well.

1. If you have a high-powered blender, you can skip to step 2. If you do not have a high-powered blender, you will want to soften your cashews to ensure that they can blend into a smooth and creamy cheese sauce. To soften the cashews, you can either boil or soak them.

Boil the cashews (the fast method): Place the cashews in a small pot, cover with water, and boil for about 10 minutes, until the cashews are very tender. Drain and rinse before using.

Soak the cashews (the slow method): Place the cashews in a bowl and cover with water. Let soak for 4 hours or overnight, until tender. Drain and rinse before using.

2. Place the cashews, plant-based milk, roasted red peppers, nutritional yeast, lemon juice, salt, onion powder, and garlic powder in your blender. Blend until completely smooth and creamy, stopping to scrape the sides as needed. Enjoy any way you like.

>>> **Make Ahead** Store leftovers in the fridge in an airtight container for up to 4 days or in the freezer for up to 4 months.

CRE

AMY

>>> Luscious creamy noodles, rich soups, silky curries—you can find all the creaminess you've ever desired in this chapter. No cows needed. Many of these recipes call for cashews or full-fat coconut milk; if you need to substitute these ingredients, check out page 10 for the best options.

Creamy Linguini Alfredo

You don't need dairy to enjoy a super silky, garlicky, dreamy alfredo sauce! This sauce is quick and easy to whip up, and I think it tastes even better than the traditional version.

SERVES: 4–6	PREP TIME: 5 MINUTES	COOK TIME: 20 MINUTES (PLUS SOFTENING TIME, IF NEEDED)

TOTAL TIME: 25 MINUTES (PLUS SOFTENING TIME, IF NEEDED)

1 cup (250 mL) raw cashews

1 lb (454 g) linguini (gluten-free if preferred)

¼ cup (60 mL) vegan butter

1 yellow onion, chopped

4 cloves garlic, minced

1¼ cups (310 mL) water

6 Tbsp (90 mL) nutritional yeast

1 tsp salt

½ tsp Italian seasoning

¼ tsp black pepper

Note

You can sub cashews with blanched almonds, macadamia nuts, or raw sunflower seeds. If using one of these subs, make sure to soften them first by boiling in water for 10–15 minutes.

1. If you have a high-powered blender, you can skip to step 2. If you do not have a high-powered blender, you will need to soften the cashews first to ensure that they become smooth and creamy. To do this, place the cashews in a small pot and cover with water. Bring to a boil and cook for about 10 minutes, until the cashews are tender. Drain and rinse before using.

2. Bring a large pot of water to a boil and cook the pasta according to the package directions.

3. Melt the butter in a pot or frying pan over medium-low heat. Add the onions and garlic and gently sauté until the onions have softened but not browned, 5–10 minutes. Remove from the heat

4. Place the onions and garlic mixture in a blender along with the water, cashews, nutritional yeast, and salt. Blend until completely smooth and creamy, stopping to scrape the sides as needed. Add the Italian seasoning and black pepper and pulse just a few times to mix in.

5. Return the hot cooked pasta to the pot, pour the alfredo sauce over the pasta, and toss well to evenly coat.

>>> Make Ahead You can prepare the sauce ahead of time and store in an airtight container in the fridge for up to 3 days or in the freezer for up to 4 months. Allow to warm to room temp before tossing with hot pasta when ready to enjoy.

Creamy Sunflower Spinach Dip

The perfect party appetizer that everyone loves! Prep it ahead of time and then just pop it in the oven to bake when you're ready to serve it. Sunflower seeds make this dip super creamy and lush while keeping it totally nut-free.

SERVES: 6–8	PREP TIME: 10 MINUTES	COOK TIME: 35 MINUTES	TOTAL TIME: 45 MINUTES

1¼ cups (310 mL) raw sunflower seeds

1 Tbsp (15 mL) olive oil

1 small yellow onion, chopped

6 cloves garlic, minced or pressed

1–1¼ cups (250–310 mL) plant-based milk (such as oat or soy)

¼ cup (60 mL) nutritional yeast

1 tsp salt

¼ tsp black pepper

5 oz (142 g) frozen chopped spinach, thawed and water squeezed out

¼ cup (60 mL) panko breadcrumbs (gluten-free if preferred)

½ tsp smoked paprika

Tortilla chips, pita triangles, or veggies, for dipping

1. Preheat your oven to 375°F (190°C).

2. Place the sunflower seeds in a pot and cover them with water. Bring to a boil and cook for about 15 minutes, until tender. Drain and rinse well. Set aside.

3. Heat the olive oil in a nonstick pan over medium-high heat. Add the onions and garlic and sauté until the onions turn translucent and begin to brown, about 5 minutes.

4. In a blender, combine the softened sunflower seeds, sautéed onions and garlic, 1 cup (250 mL) plant-based milk, nutritional yeast, salt, and pepper. Blend until completely smooth and creamy, stopping to scrape the sides as needed. If the mixture is too thick, add a bit more plant-based milk, 1 Tbsp (15 mL) at a time, to reach the desired consistency (do not add more than ¼ cup/60 mL).

5. Pour the mixture into an oven-safe 4-cup baking dish, and stir in the spinach. Evenly sprinkle with panko and paprika if desired.

6. Bake for 10–15 minutes, until heated through and the panko is golden. Serve with tortilla chips, pita triangles, or veggies.

>>> **Make Ahead** Prepare the dip without the topping, then cover it and store in the fridge for up to 3 days. When ready to enjoy, add the topping, if desired, then bake. It may take a few more minutes to bake in the oven. Alternatively, freeze the unbaked dip (without the topping) in an airtight container for up to 4 months. Thaw completely before baking.

Note

You can substitute the sunflower seeds with raw cashews, blanched almonds, or macadamia nuts. If using these nut or seed options, boil them for 15 minutes to ensure they are softened and will blend well.

Note

You can substitute the cashews with macadamia nuts, blanched almonds, or raw sunflower seeds. Note that these nuts and seeds may take a little longer to soften and will provide a slightly different taste and consistency to the soup. You could also omit the cashews and water and instead stir in 1 can (13½ fl oz/400 mL) full-fat coconut milk after blending the soup.

Four Heads of Garlic Soup

If you're a vampire, run! If you love garlic, then this soup is for you! Four roasted heads of garlic make this soup super garlicky, slightly sweet, and completely decadent. I like to add chopped kale for some texture and chew, but feel free to swap it out for another dark leafy green, such as spinach, or omit altogether.

SERVES: 8	PREP TIME: 10 MINUTES	COOK TIME: 1 HOUR 5 MINUTES	TOTAL TIME: 1 HOUR 15 MINUTES

FOR THE ROASTED GARLIC

4 heads garlic

4 tsp olive oil

Salt and black pepper

FOR THE SOUP

1 Tbsp (15 mL) olive oil

1 yellow onion, chopped

4 cups (1 L) vegetable broth or vegan chickenless broth

1 cup (250 mL) water

1 cup (250 mL) raw cashews (see note)

¼ cup (60 mL) nutritional yeast

¼ tsp salt

¼ tsp black pepper

4 cups (1 L) shredded kale (about 2½ oz/71 g), tough ribs removed

1. Preheat your oven to 400°F (200°C).

2. Roast the garlic: Slice off just the tops of the garlic bulbs so that the cloves are revealed inside. Place all four bulbs open side up on a large square of foil. Pour 1 tsp oil over each bulb, and sprinkle each with a little salt and pepper. Wrap them up in the foil, place on a baking sheet, and roast for 40 minutes, until the cloves are very soft. Allow the garlic heads to cool so you can handle them more easily.

3. Make the soup: In a large soup pot, heat the oil over medium high heat. Add the onions and sauté for about 5 minutes, until they soften and begin to brown. Add the broth, water, cashews, nutritional yeast, salt, and pepper and bring to a simmer. Cook for about 15 minutes, until the cashews are softened.

4. Working in batches, carefully transfer the soup to a blender, being careful not to overfill the blender so that it doesn't erupt. Squeeze the garlic out of the skins and add to the blender as well. Blend until completely smooth and creamy. Alternatively, an immersion blender will work in a pinch, but I generally prefer a standing blender as it usually does a better job of blending the cashews into a smooth cream.

5. Return the soup to the pot, add the kale, and bring to a simmer. Cook for another 5 minutes, until the kale has softened. Serve hot.

>>> **Make Ahead** Allow the soup to cool, then store in an airtight container in the fridge for up to 4 days or in the freezer for up to 3 months. You can also roast the garlic ahead of time and store it in an airtight container in the fridge for up to 4 days or in the freezer for up to 6 months. Defrost before adding to the soup. This way, the soup will be super quick to prepare.

Melty Mushrooms on Mash

This super savory dish feels like some good ol' hearty pub food. Creamy mushrooms served on a bed of mashed potatoes are perfect when paired with a good beer. You can use the more common cremini or button mushrooms for this recipe, but if you want to get a little creative, try using a mushroom mix. Portobello, shiitake, oyster, or king oyster will all work wonderfully.

SERVES: 4	PREP TIME: 15 MINUTES	COOK TIME: 30 MINUTES	TOTAL TIME: 45 MINUTES

FOR THE MASH

2 lb (907 g) russet or Yukon gold potatoes, peeled and quartered

½ cup (125 mL) plant-based milk (such as oat or soy)

2 Tbsp (30 mL) vegan butter

½ tsp salt

FOR THE MUSHROOMS

2 cups (500 mL) plant-based milk (such as oat or soy)

¼ cup (60 mL) cornstarch

3 Tbsp (45 mL) nutritional yeast

2 tsp fresh thyme leaves, plus more for garnish

¾ tsp salt

½ tsp black pepper, plus more for garnish

1 Tbsp (15 mL) vegan butter

1 Tbsp (15 mL) olive oil

1½ lb (680 g) mushrooms (button, cremini, or a mushroom mix), sliced

4 cloves garlic, minced or pressed

1. Make the mash: Place the potatoes in a medium pot and cover with water. Bring to a boil and continue to boil for about 15 minutes, until the potatoes are fork-tender. Drain, then return the potatoes to the pot. Add the plant-based milk, vegan butter, and salt and use a potato masher to smash them until creamy. If your potatoes are a little dry, add a splash more plant-based milk as needed.

2. Make the mushrooms: In a large glass measuring cup or a medium bowl, whisk together the plant-based milk, cornstarch, nutritional yeast, thyme, salt, and pepper. Set aside.

3. Heat the vegan butter and oil in a large pot over medium-high heat. Add the mushrooms and garlic and cook until the mushrooms have darkened in color and released their juices, about 10 minutes, stirring occasionally. Pour in the plant-based milk mixture and cook for another 5 minutes or so, until the sauce has thickened.

4. Divide the mash among four plates and top with the mushrooms. Garnish with more thyme and black pepper.

>>> **Make Ahead** Prepare the mash and mushrooms, then allow them to cool completely before storing them separately in airtight containers in the fridge for up to 3 days. Enjoy cold, or reheat gently in the microwave.

Note

For extra-rich mashed potatoes, try swapping the plant-based milk for cashew cream (page 9), store-bought plant-based culinary cream, or full-fat coconut milk.

Tahini Pesto Pan-Fried Gnocchi

Crispy on the outside and pillowy in the middle, these pan-fried gnocchi are coated in a creamy, tangy, luxurious pesto. If you don't have gnocchi on hand, this sauce would also be perfect on freshly cooked pasta. If you like pesto, you are going to LOVE LOVE LOVE this tahini pesto!

SERVES: 4	PREP TIME: 10 MINUTES	COOK TIME: 10 MINUTES	TOTAL TIME: 20 MINUTES

FOR THE PESTO

1 oz (28 g) fresh basil leaves (about 2 cups/500 mL packed)

½ cup (125 mL) plant-based milk (such as oat or soy)

¼ cup (60 mL) nutritional yeast

¼ cup (60 mL) tahini

2 Tbsp (30 mL) lemon juice

2 Tbsp (30 mL) olive oil

2 cloves garlic, peeled

½ tsp salt

¼ tsp black pepper

FOR THE GNOCCHI

2 Tbsp (30 mL) olive oil

1 lb (454 g) prepared gnocchi (check to make sure it's vegan) (gluten-free if preferred)

1. Make the pesto: Place the basil, plant-based milk, nutritional yeast, tahini, lemon juice, olive oil, garlic, salt, and pepper in your blender. Blend until smooth and creamy, stopping to scrape the sides as needed.

2. Cook the gnocchi: Heat the oil in a large nonstick skillet over medium-high heat. Add the gnocchi and fry them, not stirring, until golden brown on the bottom and crispy, about 3 minutes. Stir, then continue to fry until the gnocchi are browned all over.

3. Pour in the creamy basil sauce and heat through, 2–3 minutes. Serve hot.

>>> Make Ahead Make the pesto ahead of time and store it in an airtight container in the fridge for up to 2 days or in the freezer for up to 6 months.

This is one of my favorite weeknight meals!

Tofu Tikka Masala

This is one of my favorite weeknight meals to make because it is so easy to prepare, lusciously creamy, and full of flavorful spices! I love to serve this on rice with a side of naan or pita. I use tofu in this recipe for the meaty part, but feel free to sub your favorite vegan chicken alternative, or you can stir in roasted cauliflower just before serving.

SERVES: 6	PREP TIME: 10 MINUTES	COOK TIME: 20 MINUTES	TOTAL TIME: 30 MINUTES

2 tsp garam masala

2 tsp chili powder

1 tsp ground cumin

1 tsp ground coriander

1 tsp turmeric

1 Tbsp (15 mL) light oil (such as canola or vegetable)

1 yellow onion, thinly sliced

4 cloves garlic, minced

1 Tbsp (15 mL) minced or grated fresh ginger

1 can (14 fl oz/398 mL) crushed tomatoes (about 1⅔ cups/ 410 mL)

1 block (12 oz/340 g) extra-firm tofu, torn into 1-inch (2.5 cm) pieces (see note)

1 tsp salt

1 can (13½ fl oz/400 mL) full-fat coconut milk

1 handful fresh cilantro, coarsely chopped, for garnish

Cooked rice, for serving

Naan or pita, for serving (check to make sure it's vegan) (gluten-free if preferred)

1. In a small bowl, mix together the garam masala, chili powder, cumin, coriander, and turmeric. Set aside.

2. Heat the oil in a large saucepan over medium-high heat. When hot, add the onions and cook for about 3 minutes, until they start to become tender. Add the garlic and ginger and continue to cook until everything begins to brown. Add the spices and toast them for 30–60 seconds, stirring constantly. Add the tomatoes, tofu, and salt. Bring to a simmer and cook for 10–15 minutes, until the sauce has darkened in color. Stir in the coconut milk and bring back to a simmer just to heat through. Garnish with cilantro and serve with rice and naan.

>>> Make Ahead This curry tastes even better the next day! Allow it to cool, then store in an airtight container in the fridge for up to 5 days or in the freezer for up to 3 months.

Note

I like to tear the tofu into chunks about 1 inch (2.5 cm) in size. Some chunks will be bigger and others will be smaller, and that's perfect! Torn tofu makes for the best chicken-like texture and grips the sauce better.

Creamy Noodle Soup

This recipe is similar to chicken noodle soup but is 1,000 times better because it's vegan and it's CREAMY! It's comforting and jammed with veg, so it's the perfect recipe to keep you warm and cozy on a chilly night. I love adding corn for little pops of sweetness and edamame for some heartiness.

SERVES: 6–8	PREP TIME: 15 MINUTES	COOK TIME: 20 MINUTES (PLUS SOFTENING TIME IF NEEDED)	TOTAL TIME: 35 MINUTES

1 cup (250 mL) raw cashews

8 cups (2 L) vegetable broth or vegan chickenless broth, divided

2 Tbsp (30 mL) olive oil

3 carrots, peeled and chopped

3 ribs celery, chopped

1 yellow onion, chopped

4 cloves garlic, minced

¼ cup (60 mL) all-purpose flour (gluten-free if preferred, see note)

2 bay leaves

1 tsp dried thyme leaves

1 tsp dried rosemary leaves

6 oz (170 g) pasta of choice (gluten-free if preferred, see note)

1 cup (250 mL) frozen corn kernels

1 cup (250 mL) frozen shelled edamame or frozen peas

Salt and black pepper, to taste

1 handful fresh parsley, coarsely chopped, for garnish

>>> Make Ahead Allow the soup to cool, then store in an airtight container in the fridge for up to 4 days.

1. If you have a high-powered blender, you can skip to step 2. If you do not have a high-powered blender, you will need to soften the cashews to ensure that they blend smoothly. To do this, place the cashews in a pot and cover with water. Bring to a boil and cook for about 10 minutes, until they are tender. Drain and rinse before using.

2. In a blender, combine 1 cup (250 mL) vegetable broth with the cashews. Blend until smooth and creamy, stopping to scrape the sides as needed. Set aside.

3. In a large soup pot, heat the oil over medium-high heat. Add the carrots, celery, onions, and garlic and sauté for about 5 minutes, until the vegetables start to brown. Sprinkle in the flour and stir to coat the veggies while cooking for another minute. Add the remaining 7 cups (1.7 L) vegetable broth, bay leaves, thyme, and rosemary and bring to a simmer. Once simmering, add the pasta and continue to simmer until the pasta is al dente, about 10 minutes, depending on your pasta shape. Stir in the corn, edamame, and cashew broth mixture and bring back to a simmer to heat through. Season to taste with salt and pepper if desired, and garnish with parsley.

Note

1) This soup tends to get thicker as it sits, so if you find your soup is too thick, just stir in some water until you reach your desired consistency. 2) To make this gluten-free, sub the all-purpose flour with a gluten-free all-purpose flour blend. Some gluten-free pastas can make the soup slimy, so if you're not using wheat pasta, I recommend cooking the pasta separately, draining, then stirring it into the soup. 3) The creaminess here comes from our favorite friend: cashews. But if you need a substitute, you can swap them for macadamia nuts, blanched almonds, raw sunflower seeds, or a vegan culinary cream or coconut milk. If using any of the nut or seed substitutes, boil them for 15 minutes to soften them before using.

Velvety Roasted Red Pepper Pasta

This pasta is not only gorgeous in color with its rosy tones, but equally if not more gorgeous in flavor. In a pinch, you can use jarred roasted red peppers, but if you have the time, I highly recommend roasting your own red peppers for the best taste (see page 12 to learn how).

SERVES: 4–6	PREP TIME: 10 MINUTES	COOK TIME: 10 MINUTES (PLUS SOFTENING TIME IF NEEDED)	TOTAL TIME: 20 MINUTES

1 cup (250 mL) raw cashews

1 lb (454 g) pasta of choice (gluten-free if preferred)

2 roasted red bell peppers (see page 12) or 1 jar (1 lb/454 g), drained

1 cup (250 mL) plant-based milk (such as oat or soy)

¼ cup (60 mL) nutritional yeast

2 cloves garlic, peeled

2 tsp Italian seasoning

½ tsp salt

Note

Cashews can be substituted with blanched almonds, macadamia nuts, or raw sunflower seeds. If using these nut or seed options, boil them for 15 minutes to ensure they are softened and will blend well.

1. If you have a high-powered blender, you can skip to step 2. If you do not have a high-powered blender, you will need to soften the cashews to ensure that they blend smoothly. To do this, place the cashews in a pot and cover with water. Bring to a boil and cook for about 10 minutes, until tender. Drain and rinse before using.

2. Bring a large pot of water to a boil and cook the pasta according to the package directions.

3. In a blender, combine the roasted red peppers, plant-based milk, cashews, nutritional yeast, garlic, Italian seasoning, and salt. Blend until smooth and creamy, stopping to scrape the sides as needed.

4. Once the pasta is cooked, return it to the pot. Add the red pepper sauce and toss well to combine. If needed, turn the burner back on to heat it through.

>>> Make Ahead Prepare the sauce and store in an airtight container in the fridge for up to 4 days or in the freezer for up to 4 months (thaw before using). Toss with hot pasta and heat through on the stove.

Broccoli Has Never Tasted So Good

CRAVINGS: CHEESY, CREAMY, MEATY
GLUTEN-FREE, MAKE AHEAD

This broccoli is coated in a creamy, cheesy sauce and topped with chewy tofu bacon bits. Now this is a fun way to get your veggies in! This dish can be served as a side, but I like to make it the star of the show by spooning it over mashed potatoes, rice, or noodles.

SERVES: 4	PREP TIME: 10 MINUTES	COOK TIME: 25 MINUTES	TOTAL TIME: 35 MINUTES

FOR THE TOFU BACON BITS
½ block (6 oz/170 g) extra-firm tofu, crumbled into small pieces
1 Tbsp (15 mL) soy sauce (gluten-free if preferred)
¼ tsp liquid smoke

FOR THE BROCCOLI
2 cups (500 mL) plant-based milk (such as oat or soy)
¼ cup (60 mL) nutritional yeast
1 tsp lemon pepper
½ tsp salt
3 Tbsp (45 mL) vegan butter
1 yellow onion, chopped
4 cloves garlic, minced or pressed
3 Tbsp (45 mL) all-purpose flour (or 1½ Tbsp/22 mL for gluten-free option)
1 lb (454 g) broccoli, cut into florets (5–6 cups/1.25–1.5 L)
Smoked paprika, for garnish (optional)

Note

Instead of broccoli, this also works great with Brussels sprouts.

1. Make the tofu bacon bits: Preheat your oven to 325°F (160°C). Lightly grease a large baking sheet.

2. In a medium bowl, combine the tofu, soy sauce, and liquid smoke and toss well to coat. Spread the tofu in a single layer on the baking sheet and bake for about 25 minutes, stirring halfway through, until the tofu is dark golden brown. Set aside.

3. Make the broccoli: While the tofu is baking, in a large measuring cup or medium bowl, whisk together the plant-based milk, nutritional yeast, lemon pepper, and salt. Set aside.

4. Melt the vegan butter in a large skillet over medium-high heat. Add the onions and garlic and sauté for about 5 minutes, until the onions turn translucent and begin to brown. Sprinkle in the flour and stir to coat the veggies. Cook the flour for about 1 minute, stirring constantly. Pour in the milk mixture, add the broccoli, and bring to a simmer. Keep the sauce at a gentle simmer and cook 5–10 minutes, until the broccoli is your desired firmness when pierced with a fork and the sauce has thickened. Sprinkle with tofu bacon bits to taste and garnish with a sprinkle of paprika if desired. (You may have extra tofu bacon bits left over, which is perfect for snacking or sprinkling on other dishes.) Serve hot with any sides you like.

>>> **Make Ahead** Cool completely, then store leftovers in an airtight container for up to 3 days.

Eggplant Thai Green Curry

This is the perfect meal for a weeknight that needs a little spicing up. It's spicy, tangy, creamy, and full of amazing veg, and I love serving it on a bed of steamed rice. This curry has layers of flavor that will make it taste like it has simmered for hours, but it secretly only takes 30 minutes to make.

SERVES: 4-6	PREP TIME: 10 MINUTES	COOK TIME: 20 MINUTES	TOTAL TIME: 30 MINUTES

1 Tbsp (15 mL) light oil (such as canola or vegetable)

1 yellow onion, chopped

4 cloves garlic, minced or pressed

1 Tbsp (15 mL) minced or grated fresh ginger

6–8 Tbsp (90–120 mL) Thai Green Curry Paste (I use an entire 4 oz/114 g jar)

1 cup (250 mL) vegetable broth

1 small eggplant or 2 Japanese eggplants, cut into 1-inch (2.5 cm) pieces

1½ cups (375 mL) snow peas

1 red bell pepper, thinly sliced

1 can (13½ fl oz/400 mL) full-fat coconut milk

Zest of 1 lime

Salt, to taste

Juice of ½ lime

1 Tbsp (15 mL) chopped fresh Thai basil (sub regular basil if needed), plus more for garnish

Cooked rice, for serving

1. Heat the oil in a large soup pot over medium-high heat. Add the onions, garlic, and ginger and sauté for about 4 minutes, until the onions turn translucent. Add the curry paste (use more or less depending on how flavorful you like your curry) and cook, stirring frequently, for 1–2 minutes, until very fragrant. Add the vegetable broth and use your spoon to scrap off any browned bits stuck to the pan.

2. Stir in the eggplant, snow peas, bell peppers, coconut milk, and lime zest and juice and bring to a simmer. Continue to simmer for 5–10 minutes, until the eggplant is nice and tender. Add salt to taste, then stir in the Thai basil just before serving. Spoon the curry over steamed rice and garnish with more basil.

>>> Make Ahead As with most curries, this tastes even better the next day. Allow the curry to cool, then store in an airtight container in the fridge for up to 3 days or in the freezer for up to 3 months.

Cream of Mushroom Soup

This 20-minute mushroom soup has a creamy twist—rich, silky coconut milk! At first I was a little uncertain if the coconut flavor would work well in this recipe. But after testing it, not only does it work, it's AMAZING! Like, wow, why is this mushroom soup so much better than any I've had before?! There's just something about the earthy mushrooms and subtle but insanely addictive creamy coconut that just works.

SERVES: 6	PREP TIME: 5 MINUTES	COOK TIME: 15 MINUTES	TOTAL TIME: 20 MINUTES

2 Tbsp (30 mL) vegan butter

1 lb (454 g) button mushrooms, sliced

1 yellow onion, chopped

3 cloves garlic, minced or pressed

¼ cup (60 mL) all-purpose flour (gluten-free if preferred)

4 cups (1 L) vegetable broth

1 can (13½ fl oz/400 mL) full-fat coconut milk

1 tsp dried thyme leaves

½ tsp salt

½ tsp black pepper

¼ tsp nutmeg

1. In a large soup pot, melt the vegan butter over medium-high heat. Add the mushrooms, onions, and garlic and sauté, stirring occasionally, until the mushrooms have softened and browned, 5–10 minutes. Sprinkle in the flour, stir in, and cook 1 minute more.

2. Pour in the broth, coconut milk, thyme, salt, pepper, and nutmeg. Use your spoon to scrape the bottom of the pan and remove any bits stuck to the bottom. Bring to a simmer and cook for about 5 minutes to thicken slightly. Serve hot.

>>> **Make Ahead** Allow the soup to cool completely, then store in an airtight container in the fridge for up to 4 days or in the freezer for up to 3 months.

CHY

>>> Crispy, crunchy, salty deliciousness. The roof of my mouth is starting to hurt just thinking of this chapter! I love a fantastically crunchy dish, whether it's something as simple as Crispy Crunchy Roasted Chickpeas (page 152) or as epic as my Buttermilk Fried Oyster Mushrooms (page 150), which are like fried chicken, but better. And don't worry—no deep fryers here. You can get a satisfying crunch without tons of bad-for-you oil or any dangerous equipment!

Crispy Mini Corn Dogs

You don't need to go to a fair to enjoy a corn dog! The corn dogs you get at the fair are usually softer, deep-fried, and not vegan. These homemade corn dogs are not only vegan, but way healthier, super crispy on the outside, and tender on the inside. This recipe has a few steps, but they are surprisingly easy to whip up for a fun treat!

SERVES: 10	**PREP TIME:** 15 MINUTES	**COOK TIME:** 16 MINUTES	**TOTAL TIME:** 31 MINUTES

5 veggie dogs, cut in half

FOR THE BATTER

1½ cups (375 mL) plant-based milk (such as oat or soy)

2 Tbsp (30 mL) ground chia or ground flax

¾ cup (185 mL) cornmeal

¾ cup (185 mL) all-purpose flour (gluten-free if preferred, see note)

1½ tsp baking powder

½ tsp baking soda

½ tsp salt

FOR ASSEMBLY

½ cup (125 mL) all-purpose flour (gluten-free if preferred)

1 cup (250 mL) panko breadcrumbs (gluten-free if preferred)

Cooking spray

Mustard or ketchup, for serving

1. Oven method: Preheat your oven to 400°F (200°C) and line a large baking sheet with parchment paper.

Air-fryer method: Preheat your air fryer to 380°F (193°C).

2. Use 10 bamboo or metal skewers, and thread each veggie dog half securely onto a skewer.

Make the Batter

3. Heat the plant-based milk in the microwave or in a small pot until warm to the touch. Whisk in the chia and set aside to thicken slightly while you prepare the rest of the batter.

4. In a medium bowl, whisk together the cornmeal, flour, baking powder, baking soda, and salt. Stir in the chia milk mixture and mix well until combined. Pour the batter into a tall drinking glass.

Assemble the Corn Dogs

5. Spread the flour over a plate or shallow bowl, and put the panko breadcrumbs into another bowl.

6. Roll a skewered veggie dog in the flour to evenly coat. Dip the floured dog into the batter in the glass, swirling if needed, to coat. Finally, dip the battered dog into the panko, rolling to coat. Repeat this process with the remaining skewered dogs, placing them on the prepared baking sheet or aside on a plate.

RECIPE CONTINUES ⟶

Cook the Corn Dogs

7. Oven method: Generously spray the tops of the corn dogs on the baking sheet with cooking spray. Bake for 16 minutes, flipping halfway through and spraying the tops with cooking spray again, until crispy.

Air-fryer method: Spray the air-fryer basket with oil, then place the corn dogs in the basket in a single layer (you may need to cook them in batches). Spray the corn dogs generously with cooking spray and air-fry for 8 minutes, flipping halfway through and spraying with more cooking spray, until golden and crispy.

8. Serve hot with mustard and/or ketchup.

>>> **Make Ahead** Leftover veggie dogs can be stored in an airtight container in the fridge for up to 2 days or in the freezer for up to 2 months. Thaw completely, then reheat in the air fryer for about 5 minutes or in your oven for about 10 minutes, using the same temperatures listed in the recipe.

Takeout Tofu Sandwich

Marinated tofu in a crispy, seasoned coating gets baked (or air-fried) for the crispiest amazing sandwich that tastes like takeout food (in the best possible way). Layer this on a bun with your favorite toppings to enjoy tofu like you've never had it before! If you don't feel like a sandwich, you can also just enjoy this tofu with some mashed potatoes and greens.

SERVES: 6	PREP TIME: 15 MINUTES (PLUS MARINATING TIME)	COOK TIME: 16–20 MINUTES

TOTAL TIME: 31–35 MINUTES (PLUS MARINATING TIME)

FOR THE MARINADE

¾ cup (185 mL) plant-based milk (such as oat or soy)

1½ Tbsp (22 mL) nutritional yeast

1½ Tbsp (22 mL) soy sauce (gluten-free if preferred)

½ Tbsp Frank's RedHot Original Cayenne Pepper Sauce or similar hot sauce

½ Tbsp apple cider vinegar

½ tsp garlic powder

½ tsp onion powder

1 block (12 oz/340 g) extra-firm tofu, drained and sliced into 6 squares

FOR THE COATING

½ cup (125 mL) all-purpose flour (gluten-free if preferred)

1 cup (250 mL) panko breadcrumbs (gluten-free if preferred)

1½ tsp salt

1½ tsp paprika

1½ tsp onion powder

1½ tsp garlic powder

¾ tsp black pepper

Cooking spray

Marinate the Tofu

1. In a sealable bag or dish, mix together the plant-based milk, nutritional yeast, soy sauce, hot sauce, vinegar, garlic powder, and onion powder. Add the tofu and turn to coat each slice. Let the tofu marinate for a minimum of 30 minutes or overnight in the fridge.

Oven method: When you are ready to cook the tofu, preheat your oven to 400°F (200°C). Line a large baking sheet with parchment paper or lightly grease it.

Air-fryer method: Preheat your air fryer to 370°F (188°C).

Coat the Tofu

2. Separate the marinade from the tofu and pour the marinade into a bowl.

3. Place the flour in another bowl. In a third bowl, mix the panko with the salt, paprika, onion powder, garlic powder, and pepper.

4. Take one slice of marinated tofu and dip it into the flour. Shake off the excess flour. Dip it back into the marinade, then finally dip it into the panko mixture, evenly coating it. Place the coated tofu on the prepared baking sheet. Repeat with all the tofu slices to coat. Spray the top of the tofu slices with cooking spray so that there are no dry spots.

RECIPE CONTINUES ⟶

6 burger buns (gluten-free if
preferred)

Lettuce, pickles, tomatoes,
onions, ketchup, mustard,
vegan mayonnaise, or any
of your favorite toppings

Note

The tofu slices may look a
bit thin when you first slice
them, but they puff up when
cooking.

Cook the Tofu

5. Oven method: Bake for 10 minutes, flip, spray with more oil to
cover any dry spots, and bake for another 5–10 minutes, until they
are evenly browned and crispy.

Air-fryer method: Air-fry the slices in a single layer for 8 minutes
(working in batches if needed). Flip, spray with more oil to cover any
dry spots, and air-fry for another 4–8 minutes, until they are evenly
browned and crispy.

Assemble the sandwiches

6. Assemble your sandwiches with a slice of crispy tofu on each bun
and all your favorite toppings.

>>> **Make Ahead** The tofu can be marinated ahead of time. For the best result,
I recommend coating and baking the tofu fresh so that it stays crispy. Leftover tofu
can be stored in an airtight container in the fridge for up to 3 days. Reheat in the air
fryer or oven at the same temperature as in the recipe for a few minutes until heated
through and crispy again.

Enjoy tofu like you've never had it before!

The Best Crispy Potatoes Eva!

These potatoes take a bit of time, but I promise you, every single step is totally worth it! Crispy crunchy on the outside, pillow-soft on the inside, this just might be the best potato recipe I will ever share! There, I said it. *Technically*, these potatoes feed four, but I bet one potato lover could polish them all off!

SERVES: 4	PREP TIME: 15 MINUTES	COOK TIME: 1 HOUR	TOTAL TIME: 1 HOUR 15 MINUTES

1 tsp baking soda

2 lb (907 g) Yukon gold or russet potatoes, peeled and cut into 2-inch (5 cm) chunks

¼ cup (60 mL) olive oil

½ tsp salt, plus more for garnish

¼ tsp black pepper

1 handful fresh parsley, chopped, for garnish (optional)

½ Tbsp finely chopped fresh rosemary, for garnish (optional)

1. Preheat your oven to 450°F (230°C). Lightly grease a large baking sheet.

2. Bring a large pot of water to a boil. Once boiling, add the baking soda—the water will foam. Using a slotted spoon, carefully add the potatoes to the water and bring back to a boil. Cook until tender when pierced with a knife, but not overly soft, about 10 minutes.

3. Drain the potatoes and allow them to steam off for a minute to get rid of extra moisture. Add the potatoes to a large bowl, then pour in the olive oil, salt, and black pepper and stir the potatoes to coat. You want to mix the potatoes a little aggressively so that the outside of the potatoes gets beaten up and forms a sort of mashed potato coating. It's OK if some break apart.

4. Spread the potatoes on the prepared baking sheet and bake for 20 minutes without touching them. Use a thin spatula to flip the potatoes, then return to the oven for another 15 minutes. Flip the potatoes one last time and bake another 10–15 minutes, until the potatoes are browned all over. Garnish with parsley or rosemary if desired, and an extra sprinkle of salt.

>>> **Make Ahead** Allow the potatoes to cool, then store in an airtight container in the fridge for up to 3 days. Reheat in the oven at the same temperature as in the recipe for 8–15 minutes.

Buttermilk Fried Oyster Mushrooms

Oyster mushrooms are meaty and juicy and have a cool pull-apart texture that makes them ideal as a chicken substitute. Trust me when I say, once you make a bucket of these crunchy coated mushrooms, they will soon be your go-to vegan fried chicken recipe!

SERVES: 4	PREP TIME: 10 MINUTES (PLUS MARINATING TIME)	COOK TIME: 25 MINUTES

TOTAL TIME: 35 MINUTES (PLUS MARINATING TIME)

1 cup (250 mL) plant-based milk (such as oat or soy)

1 Tbsp (15 mL) lemon juice

4 oz (114 g) oyster mushrooms, cleaned and pulled apart into large chunks

1½ cups (375 mL) all-purpose flour

1½ tsp salt

1½ tsp paprika

¾ tsp black pepper

1 tsp garlic powder

1 tsp onion powder

Cooking spray

>>> Make Ahead I highly doubt you will have any leftovers because these are so tasty, but if you do, store them in an airtight container in the fridge for up to 3 days. Reheat and crisp up in the air fryer for 5–8 minutes or in the oven for 8–15 minutes, using the same temperatures as in the recipe.

1. Oven method: Preheat your oven to 425°F (220°C). Line a large baking sheet with parchment paper or lightly grease it.

Air-fryer method: Preheat your air fryer to 370°F (188°C).

2. In a large bowl, mix the plant-based milk and lemon juice (this will result in vegan buttermilk). Add the oyster mushrooms and toss to evenly coat. Marinate in the buttermilk for 15 minutes, tossing halfway through. (The buttermilk may separate—this is totally OK. You can just whisk it back together if needed.)

3. In another large bowl, whisk together the flour, salt, paprika, pepper, garlic powder, and onion powder.

4. Take a mushroom from the buttermilk mixture and toss it in the flour mixture. Shake off the excess flour, then dunk it back into the buttermilk mixture, and then again in the flour mixture. Set aside on the prepared baking sheet in a single layer or on a plate if using the air fryer. Repeat with the remaining mushrooms, giving each a double coating.

5. Oven method: Spray the mushrooms generously with cooking spray on all sides. Bake for 10 minutes, flip, spray the tops with more oil (making sure to coat any powdery spots), and continue to cook for another 8–15 minutes, until golden brown and crispy.

6. Air-fryer method: Grease the bottom of the air-fryer basket. Lay the coated mushrooms in the basket in a single layer—do not overcrowd (you may need to work in batches). Spray the tops generously with cooking spray. Air-fry for 5 minutes, flip, spray with more oil (making sure to coat any powdery spots), and continue cooking for another 5–10 minutes, until golden brown and crispy.

Crispy Crunchy Roasted Chickpeas

CRAVINGS: CARBY, CRUNCHY, SUGARY
GLUTEN-FREE, MAKE AHEAD, ONE POT

This is my most favorite potato chip alternative, and it's actually pretty dang healthy too! Now, there are many roasted chickpea recipes out there, and if you have tried to make them before, you may have been disappointed that your chickpeas never got crispy. I'm giving you my secret hack that makes for crispy crunchy roasted chickpeas every time! The secret to getting them extra crispy is to dry-roast them first and then season them later on. Choose your favorite seasoning combo; I offer several savory combos, but I also love them as a sweet treat with cinnamon sugar topping! Enjoy roasted chickpeas as a snack, sprinkle them on popcorn for double the crunch, use them as croutons on a salad, or sprinkle them onto soup.

SERVES: 2	PREP TIME: 5 MINUTES	COOK TIME: 32–50 MINUTES	TOTAL TIME: 37–55 MINUTES

1 can (19 oz/538 g) chickpeas, drained and rinsed

1 batch seasoning mix of choice (see below)

BASIC

1 Tbsp (15 mL) olive oil

¾ tsp chili powder

½ tsp dried thyme leaves

½ tsp salt

ITALIAN

1 Tbsp (15 mL) olive oil

1 tsp dried rosemary leaves

1 tsp lemon pepper

½ tsp salt

¼ tsp garlic powder

RANCH

1 Tbsp (15 mL) olive oil

½ tsp dried thyme leaves

½ tsp onion powder

½ tsp dried dill

¼ tsp garlic powder

½ tsp salt

CHEESY

1 Tbsp (15 mL) olive oil

1 Tbsp (15 mL) nutritional yeast

½ tsp paprika

½ tsp salt

¼ tsp garlic powder

BARBECUE

1 Tbsp (15 mL) olive oil

1 tsp brown sugar

½ tsp smoked paprika

½ tsp chili powder

½ tsp garlic powder

½ tsp salt

¼ tsp black pepper

CINNAMON SUGAR (SEE NOTE)

1 Tbsp (15 mL) melted vegan butter

2 Tbsp (30 mL) white sugar

1 tsp cinnamon

Oven Method

1. Preheat your oven to 375°F (190°C).

2. Spread the chickpeas in a single layer on an ungreased baking sheet. It's OK if they are still a bit wet; they will dry out in the oven. Bake for 30–35 minutes, stopping to shake the pan every now and then, until the chickpeas are dry and crispy. (Shaking the pan once or twice while baking will help the chickpeas dry out properly.) Remove from the oven and carefully add the hot chickpeas to a bowl along with the seasoning mix of choice. Toss well to coat the chickpeas evenly.

3. Spread the seasoned chickpeas back onto the baking sheet and return to the oven for another 10–15 minutes, until they are golden and crispy. You can snack on them still warm or wait until they're completely cooled (see note).

Air-Fryer Method

1. Preheat your air fryer to 350°F (175°C).

2. Add the chickpeas to the air fryer. It's OK if they are still a bit wet; they will dry out in the fryer. Bake for 20 minutes, stopping to shake the air fryer basket every now and then. (Shaking the basket once or twice will help the chickpeas dry out properly and get crispy.) Remove from the air-fryer and carefully add the hot chickpeas to a bowl along with the seasoning mix of choice. Toss well to coat the chickpeas evenly.

3. Return the chickpeas to the air fryer and cook for another 8–12 minutes, until they are golden and crispy. You can snack on them still warm or once they're completely cooled (see note).

>>> **Make Ahead** Store prepared and cooled chickpeas in an airtight container in the fridge for about a week. They may start to get a little soft and less crispy.

Note

When making the cinnamon sugar chickpeas, keep a close eye on them while baking, as sugar can burn quickly, and let them cool completely before enjoying, as hot sugar can burn your fingers.

Ranch Chickpeas

Cheesy Chickpeas

Barbecue Chickpeas

Cinnamon Sugar
Chickpeas

Italian Chickpeas

Crispy Buffalo Cauliflower

I'm sure you've had cauliflower wings before, but I don't think you've had them like this! The key to making this cauliflower super crunchy on the outside is to coat it in a seasoned corn-flake crush. These are the healthier (and better-tasting) alternative to chicken wings. The perfect treat to enjoy on game night, bar night, or really any night, since they are so healthy!

SERVES: 4	PREP TIME: 20 MINUTES	COOK TIME: 20-25 MINUTES	TOTAL TIME: 40-45 MINUTES

½ cup (125 mL) all-purpose flour (gluten-free if preferred)

2 Tbsp (30 mL) ground chia or ground flax

¾ cup (185 mL) warm water

4 cups (1 L) corn flakes

½ tsp garlic powder

½ tsp smoked paprika

½ tsp salt

¼ tsp black pepper

1 small head cauliflower, cut into florets

½ cup (125 mL) Frank's RedHot Original Cayenne Pepper Sauce or similar hot sauce

3 Tbsp (45 mL) vegan butter, melted

>>> **Make Ahead** Store leftovers in an airtight container in the fridge for up to 3 days. Reheat in the oven or air fryer at the same temperature as in the recipe for a few minutes until crispy. Warm the buffalo sauce in the microwave or a small pot.

1. Oven method: Preheat your oven to 400°F (200°C). Line a baking sheet with parchment paper.

Air-fryer method: Preheat your oven to 370°F (188°C).

2. Grab three big bowls. In the first bowl, place the flour. In the second bowl, mix together the chia and water.

3. Place the corn flakes, garlic powder, smoked paprika, salt, and pepper in a food processor. Pulse several times until the mixture is broken down but still has some texture. Pour the mixture into the last bowl.

4. Rinse your cauliflower florets so they are wet. Drop a handful of florets in the flour and toss to coat. Once coated, place them in the chia mixture and toss to coat. Finally, toss them in the corn-flake mixture. Spread them out on the prepared baking sheet so that they aren't touching. Repeat with all of the florets.

5. Oven method: Bake for 20–25 minutes, until golden brown and crusty and the cauliflower is tender all the way through when pierced with a knife.

Air-fryer method: Grease the air-fryer basket with cooking spray. Spread the cauliflower in a single layer, working in batches if needed. Air-fry for 15–20 minutes, flipping the cauliflower halfway through, until it is tender all the way through. You can test doneness by piercing a floret with a knife.

6. While the cauliflower is cooking, make the buffalo sauce. Place the hot sauce and vegan butter in a small bowl and stir to combine. You can pour the buffalo sauce directly on the cauliflower, but it will soften the crust. If you want to keep them super crispy, simply serve the buffalo sauce on the side and dip as you go.

Crunchy Tahini Slaw

Do you crave salad too, or am I alone on that one? Get your jaw ready for a workout because this slaw is SUPER crunchy and I'm all for it. The crunch in this is SO satisfying and the creamy tahini dressing makes this salad taste almost like comfort food. Bonus points: if you have a food processor with grating and shredding attachments, this is pretty darn quick and easy to toss together as well!

SERVES: 6–8	**PREP TIME:** 15 MINUTES	**TOTAL TIME:** 15 MINUTES

FOR THE CREAMY TAHINI DRESSING

⅓ cup (80 mL) tahini (see note)

3 Tbsp (45 mL) lemon juice
(from 1 large lemon)

2 Tbsp (30 mL) water

1 Tbsp (15 mL) Dijon mustard

½ Tbsp agave or maple syrup

1 clove garlic, minced or pressed

½ tsp salt

¼ tsp black pepper

FOR THE SLAW

4 cups (1 L) shredded cabbage
(purple, white, or a combo)

1 cup (250 mL) peeled and
grated carrots (from about
2 carrots)

1 cup (250 mL) finely chopped
broccoli florets

1 cup (250 mL) chopped sugar
snap peas

1 cup (250 mL) coarsely chopped
fresh cilantro

¼ cup (60 mL) roasted, salted
peanuts, coarsely chopped

4 green onions, chopped

1. Make the creamy tahini dressing: In a small bowl, combine the tahini, lemon juice, water, mustard, agave, garlic, salt, and pepper and mix well. Set aside.

2. Assemble the slaw: In a large bowl, combine the cabbage, carrots, broccoli, peas, and cilantro. Drizzle with as much tahini dressing as desired and toss well. (I like to start with about half the dressing and add more, to taste, if needed.) Garnish with peanuts and green onions and enjoy!

>>> **Make Ahead** Prep the dressing and slaw and store separately in airtight containers in the fridge. The slaw will last for up to 3 days and the dressing for 1 week. Dress the salad before serving. If you have leftover tahini dressing, it's great as a veggie dip!

Note

If you want to substitute the tahini, try using cashew butter or almond butter instead for another great variation!

Extra-Crispy Onion Rings

I LOVE onion rings, but I'm really not a fan of deep-fried food, so these baked onion rings are my dream! These are extra crispy without the need for a ton of oil. They are easy to whip up and can be made in the oven or air fryer. I love enjoying mine with ketchup (hello, comfort food), but of course you could serve them alongside a burger, sandwich, or any vegan meaty-type dish.

SERVES: 4	**PREP TIME:** 10 MINUTES	**COOK TIME:** 7–15 MINUTES	**TOTAL TIME:** 17–25 MINUTES

1 cup (250 mL) plant-based milk (such as oat or soy)

1¼ cups (310 mL) all-purpose flour (gluten-free if preferred)

1 tsp paprika

1 tsp salt

½ tsp garlic powder

2 cups (500 mL) panko breadcrumbs (gluten-free if preferred)

1 large sweet onion, sliced into ½-inch (1.2 cm) slices and separated into rings

Cooking spray

1. Oven method: Preheat your oven to 425°F (220°C). Lightly grease a large baking sheet.

Air-fryer method: Preheat your air fryer to 400°F (200°C).

2. In a medium bowl, mix together the plant-based milk, flour, paprika, salt, and garlic powder until combined. Place the panko in a second medium bowl.

3. Using small tongs, dunk one onion ring into the wet batter, coating it nicely, then dip it into the panko, coating it well. (I find it's easiest to use tongs to avoid goopy fingers.) Place the coated onion ring on the prepared baking sheet or on a large plate if using an air fryer. Repeat with the remaining onion rings.

4. Oven method: Spray the onion rings with oil, then bake for 10 minutes. Flip and spray with more cooking spray, then bake for another 5 minutes until golden brown on both sides.

Air-fryer method: Spray the air-fryer basket and the onion rings with cooking spray. Place the onion rings in a single layer in the air-fryer basket. Air-fry for about 7 minutes, until golden brown and crispy—no need to flip.

Nacho Taco Bowls

CRAVINGS: CARBY, CREAMY, CRUNCHY, MEATY
GLUTEN-FREE, MAKE AHEAD

I know this recipe has more ingredients than I usually opt for, but don't be intimidated—every step is easy to prepare and you can mix and match your taco bowl fillings. First you have the nacho-seasoned taco bowls, which are crispy and chewy and taste amazing! Then you have my chipotle black beans, which are savory, spicy, and bursting with flavor. Last is my creamy cumin dressing, which is simple to make and a great multipurpose dressing you can use on salads or as a dip for Garlic Herb Potato Wedges (page 62) or veggies. YUM!

SERVES: 4	**PREP TIME:** 20 MINUTES	**COOK TIME:** 25 MINUTES (PLUS SOFTENING TIME, IF NEEDED)

TOTAL TIME: 45 MINUTES (PLUS SOFTENING TIME, IF NEEDED)

FOR THE NACHO TACO BOWL

2 Tbsp (30 mL) olive oil or cooking spray

1 Tbsp (15 mL) nutritional yeast

½ tsp chili powder

¼ tsp onion powder

¼ tsp garlic powder

¼ tsp salt

4 large tortillas (wheat, corn, or gluten-free)

FOR THE CHIPOTLE BLACK BEANS

1 Tbsp (15 mL) light oil (such as canola or vegetable)

1 yellow onion, chopped

4 cloves garlic, minced or pressed

1 chipotle pepper in adobo sauce, chopped

1 tsp ground cumin

1 tsp dried oregano leaves

½ tsp salt

1 can (19 oz/538 g) black beans, drained and rinsed

½ cup (125 mL) salsa (mild, medium, or hot)

1. Make the nacho taco bowls: Preheat your oven to 375°F (190°C). Place four oven-safe bowls upside down on a large baking sheet and brush the outside of the bowls with oil or spray with cooking spray. (You may need to use two baking sheets, depending on the size of your bowls.)

2. In a small bowl, mix together the nutritional yeast, chili powder, onion powder, garlic powder, and salt. Brush one side of each tortilla with a bit of oil or lightly spray it with oil. Sprinkle 1 tsp seasoning mixture evenly over the oiled tortillas.

3. Drape the seasoned tortillas over the prepared upside-down bowls, seasoned side up. Bake for 10–15 minutes, until the tortillas are golden brown. Allow to cool for 5 minutes before removing from the bowls.

4. Make the chipotle black beans: Heat the oil in a large skillet. Add the onions and garlic and sauté until the onions turn translucent and begin to brown, about 5 minutes. Add the chipotle peppers, cumin, oregano, and salt and cook, stirring often, for another minute. Add the black beans and salsa and heat through, about 5 minutes more. If the mixture gets too thick, just add a splash of water.

5. Make the creamy cumin dressing: If you have a high-powered blender, skip to step 6. If you do not have a high-powered blender, you will need to soften the cashews first. To do so, place them in a small pot and cover with water. Bring to a boil and cook for 10 minutes. Drain and rinse.

RECIPE CONTINUES ⟶

FOR THE CREAMY CUMIN DRESSING

1 cup (250 mL) raw cashews

¾ cup (185 mL) water

3 Tbsp (45 mL) lemon juice

1 tsp ground cumin

½ tsp salt

1 clove garlic, minced or pressed

FOR ASSEMBLY (FEEL FREE TO SUB WITH YOUR FAVORITE TACO SALAD FILLINGS)

4 cups (1 L) chopped romaine lettuce

1 cup (250 mL) cooked rice (white or brown)

1 cup (250 mL) sliced cherry tomatoes

1 avocado, peeled, pitted, and sliced

½ cup (125 mL) corn kernels (thawed if frozen)

1 handful fresh cilantro, coarsely chopped

1 lime, sliced into wedges

½ cup (125 mL) salsa

6. Place the cashews, water, lemon juice, cumin, salt, and garlic in a blender and blend until completely smooth and creamy, stopping to scrape the sides as needed.

7. Assemble the taco bowls: Divide the lettuce evenly among the taco bowls to coat the bottom and to stop the bowls from getting soggy. Top the lettuce with the black beans, rice, cherry tomatoes, avocados, and corn. Drizzle with the dressing to taste, and garnish with cilantro, lime wedges, and extra salsa.

>>> **Make Ahead** The taco bowls, chipotle beans, and cumin dressing can all be made ahead of time and stored separately in airtight containers. Store the taco bowls at room temperature for up to 2 days. The beans will keep for up to 4 days in the fridge, and the dressing should keep for up to a week in the fridge. Assemble the taco bowls fresh.

One-of-a-Kind Eggplant Parm

This eggplant parmesan is like no other you've ever had. The eggplant is baked (not fried) in an extra-crunchy corn-flake crust! As with my Crispy Buffalo Cauliflower (page 157), I find that substituting breadcrumbs with corn flakes makes things extra crispy! Who knew this common breakfast cereal could be the secret to the ultimate crunch? I also include a simple tomato sauce recipe, but feel free to swap it for a jarred tomato sauce if you're feeling lazy. You can also top the eggplant with my Sunflower Parmesan (page 107) or Creamy Potato Cheese Sauce (page 112) to make it cheesy, but I often just serve it plain. I like to serve this on its own with a salad, but it's equally delicious with pasta.

SERVES: 4–6	PREP TIME: 15 MINUTES	COOK TIME: 35 MINUTES	TOTAL TIME: 50 MINUTES

FOR THE SIMPLE TOMATO SAUCE

1 Tbsp (15 mL) olive oil

1 yellow onion, chopped

4 cloves garlic, minced or pressed

1 can (28 fl oz/796 mL) whole tomatoes

1 tsp dried oregano leaves

¼ tsp salt

¼ tsp crushed red pepper flakes (optional for spice)

FOR THE CORN-FLAKE COATING

6 cups (1.5 L) corn flakes (gluten-free if preferred)

6 Tbsp (90 mL) nutritional yeast

1½ tsp paprika

¾ tsp onion powder

¾ tsp garlic powder

¾ tsp black pepper

¾ tsp salt

1. Preheat your oven to 375°F (190°C) and lightly grease a large baking sheet or line it with parchment paper.

2. Make the simple tomato sauce: Heat the oil in a large skillet or saucepan over medium-high heat. Add the onions and garlic and sauté for about 5 minutes, until the onions turn translucent and begin to brown. Add the tomatoes, oregano, salt, and red pepper flakes (if using). Use a potato masher to mash the tomatoes into a sauce texture. (I find that using canned whole tomatoes and mashing them like this make for the best sauce texture as opposed to buying diced tomatoes.) Bring the sauce to a simmer and cook for about 20 minutes, until the sauce has darkened in color and thickened slightly. While the sauce simmers, you can move onto the next steps.

3. Make the corn-flake coating: Place the corn flakes, nutritional yeast, paprika, onion powder, garlic powder, pepper, and salt in a food processor. Pulse several times until the corn flakes have broken down but there is still some texture. Pour the corn-flake mixture into a large flat bowl.

4. Make the batter: In a second large flat bowl, whisk together the plant-based milk, flour, nutritional yeast, and salt until combined.

RECIPE CONTINUES ⟶

FOR THE BATTER

1½ cups (375 mL) plant-based milk (such as oat or soy)

¾ cup (185 mL) all-purpose flour (gluten-free if preferred)

3 Tbsp (45 mL) nutritional yeast

½ tsp salt

FOR ASSEMBLY

1 large eggplant, cut into 1-inch-thick (2.5 cm) rounds

Cooking spray

1 small handful fresh basil leaves, for garnish (optional)

Sunflower Parmesan (page 107), for garnish (optional)

Creamy Potato Cheese Sauce (page 112), for garnish (optional)

5. Assemble the eggplant parm: Using tongs, take an eggplant round and dip it into the batter to coat it, then dip it in the corn-flake mixture to coat. Place on the prepared baking sheet. Repeat with all the eggplant rounds.

6. Lightly spray both sides of the coated eggplant slices with cooking spray, then bake for about 25 minutes (no need to flip) until the corn-flake crust is golden brown. Serve hot with the tomato sauce and any garnishes you desire.

>>> *Make Ahead* This recipe is best served fresh, but you can store the eggplant parm and tomato sauce separately, once cooled, in airtight containers in the fridge for up to 3 days. Reheat the eggplant in the oven at the same temperature as in the recipe until heated through, about 10 minutes. The sauce can be reheated on the stove.

Crunchy Roasted Munchies

Warning: you will not be able to stop munching on these sweet, salty, and spicy nuts and pretzels! These are the perfect party snack, ideal for munching on while watching a movie, or handy for taking on-the-go. If you happen to leave a bowl of these out on the table for passersby to enjoy, they'll be gone by the end of the day! I speak from experience.

SERVES: 6	PREP TIME: 5 MINUTES	COOK TIME: 20 MINUTES	TOTAL TIME: 25 MINUTES

¾ cup (185 mL) raw almonds

¾ cup (185 mL) raw walnuts

½ cup (125 mL) raw sunflower seeds

3 Tbsp (45 mL) brown sugar

1 Tbsp (15 mL) melted vegan butter

1 Tbsp (15 mL) maple syrup

½ tsp ground cumin

½ tsp salt

¼ tsp cayenne (optional for spice)

2 cups (500 mL) small pretzels (gluten-free if preferred)

Note

The combo of almonds, walnuts, and sunflower seeds is my favorite, but feel free to substitute other nuts and seeds.

1. Preheat your oven to 350°F (175°C). Line a large baking sheet with parchment paper or lightly grease it.

2. Spread the almonds, walnuts, and sunflower seeds evenly over the baking sheet. Bake for 10 minutes, then remove from the oven.

3. In a large bowl, mix together the brown sugar, vegan butter, maple syrup, cumin, salt, and cayenne. Add the pretzels and hot almonds, walnuts, and sunflower seeds, and mix well to evenly coat. (The sauce will sizzle when you add the hot nuts.) Spread on the baking sheet and bake for another 10 minutes, stopping to give everything a stir halfway through, until the nuts are golden brown. Remove from the oven and allow to cool completely, then transfer to a serving dish, snapping any large chunks apart.

>>> **Make Ahead** Allow to cool completely, then store in an airtight container at room temperature for up to 2 weeks (although I bet it won't last that long!).

ICY

>>> If you're like me, then you love a good mouth-burning sizzle every now and then. Especially when the temperature outside is below zero, I love a hot and spicy dish to warm me up! For most of these recipes, I've given a range of how much spice to add to the dish. If you like it hot hot hot, then feel free to add the max or even more if you like. If you are a bit timid when it comes to spice, aim for the lesser amount. For anyone who doesn't like any spice at all, you can still enjoy this chapter by omitting the spice completely!

Sriracha Roasted Eggplant

You may think of veggies as a side dish, but this creamy roasted eggplant is so bursting with tangy, spicy flavor, it will be the star of the show! This recipe is my take on nasu dengaku, which is a traditional Japanese dish. Serve with rice and a side of greens for a gorgeous dinner. You can dig out the eggplant flesh with a fork if you like, but the skin gets so tender when preparing the eggplant this way, I recommend eating the skin as well!

SERVES: 4	PREP TIME: 15 MINUTES	COOK TIME: 45 MINUTES	TOTAL TIME: 1 HOUR

FOR THE EGGPLANT

2 medium eggplants

1 Tbsp (15 mL) light oil (such as canola or vegetable), for brushing

Pinch of salt

FOR THE SPICY MISO SAUCE

3 Tbsp (45 mL) white miso paste

1 Tbsp (15 mL) sriracha (see spice level)

1 Tbsp (15 mL) soy sauce (gluten-free if preferred)

½ Tbsp agave or maple syrup

½ Tbsp rice vinegar

2 tsp toasted sesame oil

1 Tbsp (15 mL) minced or grated fresh ginger

2 cloves garlic, minced or pressed

FOR GARNISH

2 green onions, chopped

1 Tbsp (15 mL) toasted sesame seeds

1. Preheat your oven to 400°F (200°C). Lightly grease a large baking sheet or line it with parchment paper.

2. **Prepare the eggplants:** Slice your eggplants in half lengthwise (you can leave the stem on for decoration). Use the tip of your knife to score the eggplant flesh diagonally to make a diamond pattern. Be careful not to cut through the skin. Brush the scored eggplants with oil and sprinkle with salt.

3. **Make the spicy miso sauce:** In a medium bowl, whisk together the miso paste, sriracha, soy sauce, agave, rice vinegar, sesame oil, ginger, and garlic.

4. **Bake the eggplant:** Place the eggplant halves cut side up on the prepared baking sheet and bake for 25–30 minutes, until the eggplants are very tender. Turn the oven up to 450°F (230°C). Spread the spicy miso sauce evenly over the eggplant halves and return to the oven. Bake for another 10–15 minutes, until the sauce is bubbling and browned. Garnish with green onions and sesame seeds. Serve hot.

>>> *Make Ahead* I love these served hot, but they are also delicious served cold. Allow the cooked eggplant to cool, then store in an airtight container in the fridge for up to 3 days. Leftovers also work well as a dip. Just mash up the eggplant and serve with tortilla chips.

>>> *Spice Level* If you don't like spice, omit the sriracha. This will still be a delicious recipe! If you like extra spice, add more sriracha to taste.

Firecracker Cauliflower

CRAVINGS: CARBY, SPICY, SUGARY
GLUTEN-FREE, MAKE AHEAD

Sticky, sweet, spicy, and juicy. If you are on the fence about cauliflower, this is the recipe that will convert you! This easy-to-make dinner is a go-to for me when I'm craving takeout vibes. Serve this cauliflower on a bed of fluffy steamed rice and you're in for a firecrackin' good time!

SERVES: 4	PREP TIME: 10 MINUTES	COOK TIME: 33 MINUTES	TOTAL TIME: 43 MINUTES

FOR THE CAULIFLOWER

1 head cauliflower (about 2 lb/907 g), cut into florets

1 Tbsp (15 mL) light oil (such as canola or vegetable)

2 cloves garlic, minced or pressed

¼ tsp salt

¼ tsp black pepper

FOR THE FIRECRACKER SAUCE

½ cup (125 mL) brown sugar

⅓ cup (80 mL) Frank's RedHot Original Cayenne Pepper Sauce or similar hot sauce (see spice level)

¼ cup (60 mL) water

2 Tbsp (30 mL) cornstarch

1 Tbsp (15 mL) rice vinegar

¼ tsp crushed red pepper flakes, or more to taste (see spice level)

FOR ASSEMBLY

2 cups (500 mL) cooked rice or grain of preference

¼ cup (60 mL) sliced green onions

1. Preheat your oven to 450°F (230°C). Lightly grease a large baking sheet.

2. Make the cauliflower: Place the cauliflower in a large mixing bowl along with the oil, garlic, salt, and pepper. Toss well to evenly coat the cauliflower. Spread the cauliflower on the prepared baking sheet, making sure to space the florets out as much as possible. Bake for about 25 minutes, flipping halfway through, until the cauliflower is tender and browned.

3. Make the firecracker sauce: While the cauliflower is baking, place the brown sugar, hot sauce, water, cornstarch, rice vinegar, and red pepper flakes in a small pot. Bring to a simmer and cook for about 5 minutes, whisking often, until thickened.

4. Drizzle the sauce all over the roasted cauliflower on the pan, and toss well to evenly coat the cauliflower. Return the pan to the oven and continue baking for another 4–8 minutes, until the cauliflower is sticky-delicious. Serve over rice and garnish with green onions.

>>> *Make Ahead* You can prep the cauliflower ahead of time, allow to cool completely, then store in an airtight container in the fridge for up to 3 days.

>>> *Spice Level* For a less spicy version, try substituting Frank's RedHot Original Cayenne Pepper Sauce with mild hot sauce, or with an equal amount of vegan barbecue sauce. Omit the red pepper flakes. For extra spicy, add more red pepper flakes to taste.

Peppery Udon Stir-Fry

This isn't your average stir-fry—this is something special! Inspired by Japanese cuisine, thick udon noodles are coated in a spicy black pepper sauce with boatloads of fresh veg. I love to use whatever stir-fry veggies I have on hand, such as broccoli, carrots, bell peppers, bok choy, onions, baby corn, mushrooms, zucchini, or peas. You could even grab a bag of frozen veggies! Make sure to be generous with your black pepper as this is what really makes this dish sing!

SERVES: 6	PREP TIME: 10 MINUTES	COOK TIME: 15 MINUTES	TOTAL TIME: 25 MINUTES

FOR THE BLACK PEPPER SAUCE

¼ cup (60 mL) soy sauce (gluten-free if preferred)

1½ Tbsp (22 mL) hoisin

2 Tbsp (30 mL) rice vinegar

¾ tsp black pepper (or to taste, see spice level)

FOR THE NOODLES

2 packets (each 7 oz/200 g) vacuum-packed udon noodles (see note for gluten-free)

1 Tbsp (15 mL) sesame oil

4 cups (1 L) stir-fry vegetables (like broccoli, carrots, bell peppers, bok choy, onions, baby corn, mushrooms, zucchini, or peas), chopped into bite-size pieces

Black pepper, to taste

2 green onions, chopped

Note

For gluten-free, sub the udon noodles with your favorite gluten-free noodles. I recommend a thicker noodle for the best texture.

1. Make the black pepper sauce: Place the soy sauce, hoisin, rice vinegar, and black pepper in a small bowl or large measuring cup and whisk to combine. Set aside.

2. Cook the noodles: Bring a large pot of water to a boil and cook the noodles according to the package directions.

3. Heat the sesame oil in a large skillet or nonstick frying pan over medium heat. Add the stir-fry vegetables and fry for 5–10 minutes, until the veggies are cooked and are beginning to brown. Be sure not to overcook the veg; you still want it to have some bite and texture. Add the udon noodles and the sauce and toss well to combine. Season with extra pepper, if desired, and the green onions.

>>> **Make Ahead** Allow the stir-fry to cool, then store in an airtight container in the fridge for up to 4 days. These noodles are delicious cold or hot!

>>> **Spice Level** To make this less spicy, reduce the black pepper. For extra spicy, add more black pepper to taste.

Spicy Snacky Jamaican Patty

With tofu, mushrooms, and soy sauce, there isn't much about this recipe that's traditional, but you're just going to have to trust me with this one. These Jamaican patties may not be conventional, but they sure are delicious! The mushrooms and tofu provide the perfect chewy, juicy, meaty texture, while the soy sauce helps with the color, salt, and umami. These flaky pastries are a fave in my house—I love stashing some in the freezer so that they are ready to be heated when spicy snacks are required!

MAKES: 12 PATTIES | **PREP TIME:** 20 MINUTES | **COOK TIME:** 45 MINUTES | **TOTAL TIME:** 1 HOUR 5 MINUTES

FOR THE PASTRY

3½ cups (875 mL) all-purpose flour

1 Tbsp (15 mL) white sugar

2 tsp turmeric

½ tsp salt

1 cup (250 mL) cold vegan butter, cubed

1 cup (250 mL) cold water

FOR THE FILLING

1 Tbsp (15 mL) light oil (such as canola or vegetable)

1 yellow onion, chopped

3 cloves garlic, minced

1–2 Scotch bonnet peppers, deseeded and minced (see spice level)

8 oz (227 g) mushrooms, chopped

1 block (12 oz/340 g) extra-firm tofu, drained

3 Tbsp (45 mL) soy sauce, plus more to taste

1 tsp smoked paprika

1 tsp dried thyme leaves

½ tsp allspice

¼ tsp black pepper

Salt, to taste

Make the Pastry

1. To make the pastry, you can either use a food processor or mix by hand.

Food processor method: Place the flour, sugar, turmeric, and salt in your food processor and pulse to combine. Add the vegan butter and pulse several times until you reach a sandy texture. Add the water and pulse until a shaggy dough forms. Turn the dough out onto a clean work surface and gather into a ball. Cover in plastic wrap and chill in the fridge for 30 minutes while you prepare the filling, or overnight.

Hand method: Place the flour, sugar, turmeric, and salt in a large bowl and whisk together. Add the vegan butter and use a pastry cutter or fork to cut the butter into the flour until you reach a sandy texture. Mix in the water until a shaggy dough forms. Turn the dough out onto a clean work surface and gather into a ball. Cover in plastic wrap and chill in the fridge for 30 minutes while you prepare the filling, or overnight.

Make the Filling

2. Heat the oil in a large cast-iron skillet or nonstick pan over medium-high heat. Add the onions, garlic, and Scotch bonnet peppers. Sauté for about 5 minutes, until the onions turn translucent and begin to brown. Add the mushrooms and continue to cook until they have darkened in color and released their juices, another 5–10 minutes.

RECIPE CONTINUES ⟶

1) A Scotch bonnet pepper will get you that classic spicy taste, but if you can't find one, sub your favorite hot pepper, such as habanero or jalapeño.
2) If you aren't up for making the pastry, the filling is delicious on its own served with rice and some greens for a Jamaican-inspired dish.
3) When working with hot peppers, always wear rubber gloves and wash your hands well.

3. Use your hands to crumble the tofu into the pan, then add the soy sauce, paprika, thyme, allspice, and pepper and mix well. Continue to cook for another 5–10 minutes, until most of the moisture is absorbed and the tofu looks browned. Add more soy sauce or some salt to taste if desired. Remove from the heat and set aside.

Assemble the Patties

4. Remove the dough from the fridge and divide into 12 even pieces. On a lightly floured work surface, roll one ball of dough into a circle about 6 inches (15 cm) in diameter. Fill the pastry with about 3 Tbsp (45 mL) tofu mushroom filling. Fold over the dough to make a half-circle shape, then use a fork to crimp the edge closed. Repeat with the remaining dough to make 12 patties.

Cook the Patties

5. Oven method: Preheat your oven to 375°F (190°C) and line two large baking sheets with parchment paper.

Air-fryer method: Preheat the air fryer to 350°F (175°C).

6. Oven method: Place the patties on the baking sheets in a single layer without touching each other. Bake for 18–23 minutes, until the patties are golden around the edges. Allow to cool for 10 minutes before serving.

Air-fryer method: Place the patties in a single layer so that they aren't overlapping (you will likely be able to cook only two patties at a time, so you'll need to cook these in batches). Air-fry for 10–15 minutes, until the patties are lightly golden. Let cool slightly before enjoying.

>>> **Make Ahead** You can assemble the patties and store them in the fridge, separated by parchment paper, for up to 2 days before baking. To freeze, lay the patties on parchment-lined baking sheets and freeze completely. Once frozen, put the patties in a sealable freezer bag or container for up to 3 months. To bake or air-fry from frozen, cook at the same temperature as in the recipe, adding about 3–5 minutes more time to make sure they are fully heated through. Store baked patties in an airtight container in the fridge for up to 2 days or in the freezer for up to 3 months.

>>> **Spice Level** If you are not a fan of spice, reduce or omit the Scotch bonnet pepper. For extra spicy use two Scotch bonnet peppers, or even more if desired.

Chili Ginger Carrot Pot Stickers

Most vegan pot sticker recipes are filled with mushrooms, and while I do love a good mushroom dish, I wanted to try something a little different, as not all of my friends like mushrooms. I always have a bag of carrots on hand, so one day I came up with this carrot filling, which quickly became one of my most favorite pot sticker fillings ever! Carrot pot stickers are spicy and bursting with ginger! Since this makes a fairly large batch, I like to eat some right away and freeze some for later. You can make the wrappers from scratch if you like, but honestly, if your grocery store sells premade wrappers, it will save you a ton of time—just double-check to make sure the ingredients are vegan.

MAKES: ABOUT 30 POT STICKERS	**PREP TIME:** 30 MINUTES (PLUS RESTING TIME FOR THE DOUGH)	**COOK TIME:** 15–25 MINUTES

TOTAL TIME: 45–55 MINUTES (PLUS RESTING TIME FOR THE DOUGH)

FOR THE DUMPLING WRAPPERS (OR SUB STORE-BOUGHT) (GLUTEN-FREE IF PREFERRED)

2¼ cups (560 mL) all-purpose flour, plus more for rolling

¾ cup (185 mL) boiling water

¼ tsp salt

Cornstarch, for dusting

FOR THE CARROT FILLING

1 Tbsp (15 mL) sesame oil

4 green onions, chopped (light and dark green parts separated)

2 Tbsp (30 mL) minced or grated fresh ginger

6 cloves garlic, minced or pressed

6 medium carrots, peeled and grated (4 cups/1 L grated)

⅓ cup (80 mL) roasted, salted peanuts, chopped

2 Tbsp (30 mL) soy sauce (gluten-free if preferred)

Make the Dumpling Wrappers (Optional)

1. Place the flour, water, and salt in the bowl of a stand mixer with a dough hook, or in a large bowl. With the mixer or spoon, mix until the dough comes together, then knead it with the dough hook or turn onto a clean work surface and knead by hand for a couple of minutes. The dough will be tough. Cover with a slightly damp clean dish towel and let the dough rest for 20–60 minutes. Resting the dough relaxes the gluten and makes it easier to roll into wrappers. In the meantime, you can prepare the carrot filling.

2. When ready to roll out the wrappers, poke a hole in the middle of the dough ball to make a doughnut shape. Use your hands to gently stretch the hole, stretching the dough out until you have a long, circular rope of dough that is about 1¼ inches (3 cm) thick. Cut the rope into 1-inch (2.5 cm) pieces, making about 30 pieces of dough.

3. Work with one dough piece at a time, covering the rest of the pieces with the damp towel while you're not using them. Use a rolling pin to roll out the dough piece into a very thin circle, 3 4 inches (8–10 cm) in diameter. When stacking the wrappers, lightly dust each wrapper with a bit of cornstarch so that they do not stick to each other. Repeat with all of the pieces of dough to make all of the wrappers. Use them fresh or place in a sealable bag and store in the fridge for up to 3 days or in the freezer for up to 1 month.

RECIPE CONTINUES ⟶

1 Tbsp (15 mL) hoisin (gluten-
free if preferred)

2–4 tsp chili garlic sauce
(see spice level)

FOR THE DIPPING SAUCE

¼ cup (60 mL) soy sauce (gluten-
free if preferred)

3 Tbsp (45 mL) rice vinegar

¼ tsp sesame oil

FOR FINISHING

Light oil, for frying (such as
canola or vegetable)

Sesame seeds, for garnish

Note

If you prefer, you can steam
or gently boil these for
about 5 minutes, instead
of frying them.

Make the Pot Stickers

4. Make the carrot filling: Heat the sesame oil in a large skillet over medium-high heat. When hot, add the white and light green parts of the green onions, the ginger, and the garlic. Sauté for 1–2 minutes, until fragrant. Add the carrots and continue to cook until the carrots are tender and have reduced but still have a bit of crunch, about 5 minutes. Remove from the heat and stir in the peanuts, soy sauce, hoisin, and chili garlic sauce to taste. Allow the filling to cool a bit before filling the wrappers.

5. Make the dipping sauce: In a small bowl, mix together the soy sauce, rice vinegar, and sesame oil.

6. Assemble the pot stickers: Place a wrapper on a clean work surface. Use your finger to brush water around the edges of the wrapper (this will help it stick). Spoon about 2–3 tsp of the carrot filling into the center of the wrapper. Fold the wrapper over to create a semicircle shape, then pinch the edges together to seal the filling inside. Repeat with the remaining filling and wrappers.

7. Cook the pot stickers: Heat about 1 Tbsp (15 mL) light oil in a nonstick pan over medium-high heat. Add the pot stickers in a single layer, leaving room around each one—you will need to work in batches. Fry without touching them for 2–3 minutes, until they are golden brown and crisp on the bottom. Add about ¼ cup (60 mL) water to the pan (be careful, as it will sizzle), and immediately cover with a lid. Cook for another 2–3 minutes to steam the tops of the pot stickers. Repeat, cooking as many dumplings as you desire. Garnish with the dark green parts of the green onions and sesame seeds, and serve with the dipping sauce.

>>> **Make Ahead** Pot stickers are best enjoyed freshly fried. If you wish to assemble them in advance, you can store them covered in the fridge for up to 2 days before frying. Assembled pot stickers can also be frozen before frying. Freeze them in a single layer on a parchment-lined baking sheet until they are solid, then transfer them to a freezer-friendly container for up to 3 months. Thaw completely before frying.

>>> **Spice Level** For a mild version, use the lesser amount of chili garlic sauce, or you could even omit it. For extra spicy, use 4 tsp chili garlic sauce, and you can even add some extra chili garlic sauce to the dipping sauce!

This is the perfect spicy
dip for game day!

Jalapeño Popper Dip

Rich, creamy, warm, and cheesy, with crunchy panko topping, this is the perfect spicy dip for game day paired with a pint of beer, or for a cozy weekend in, watching your favorite movie with friends. This one is a crowd-pleaser! Make sure you don't discard the brine in the jalapeño can as it adds a ton of spicy, tangy flavor to this dip!

SERVES: 8 | **PREP TIME:** 10 MINUTES | **COOK TIME:** 20 MINUTES (PLUS SOFTENING TIME, IF NEEDED)

TOTAL TIME: 30 MINUTES (PLUS SOFTENING TIME, IF NEEDED)

1½ cups (375 mL) raw cashews

1 cup (250 mL) water

3 Tbsp (45 mL) nutritional yeast

2 Tbsp (30 mL) brine from pickled jalapeños

1 Tbsp (15 mL) white miso paste

½ tsp onion powder

½ tsp garlic powder

1 can (6.7 oz/190 g) pickled jalapeño slices, drained and chopped (see spice level)

½ cup (125 mL) panko breadcrumbs (gluten-free if preferred)

2 Tbsp (30 mL) melted vegan butter

1 Tbsp (15 mL) nutritional yeast

¼ tsp salt

1 Tbsp (15 mL) fresh parsley, for garnish

Tortilla chips, crackers, or veggies, for serving

1. Preheat your oven to 375°F (190°C).

2. If you have a high-powered blender, you can skip straight to the next step. If you have a regular blender, you may want to soften the cashews first to ensure they blend smoothly. To do this, place them in a small pot and cover with water. Bring to a boil and cook for about 10 minutes, until the cashews are very tender. Drain and rinse with cold water before using.

3. Place the cashews, water, nutritional yeast, jalapeño brine, miso paste, onion powder, and garlic powder in a blender and blend until completely smooth and creamy, stopping to scrape the sides as needed. Pour into a 4-cup oven-safe dish and stir in the chopped jalapeños.

4. In a small bowl, mix together the panko, vegan butter, nutritional yeast, and salt. Sprinkle this over the dip and spread it evenly. Bake for 15–20 minutes, until heated through and the panko is golden brown. Garnish with parsley and serve with your favorite dippers, such as tortilla chips, crackers, or veggies.

>>> **Make Ahead** To prepare this ahead of time, prepare the recipe up to step 3. Cover the dip and store it in the fridge for up to 3 days. When ready to serve, continue with step 4 to prepare the panko topping and bake the dip fresh. It may need to bake for a few extra minutes if it was cold from the fridge. The uncooked dip without panko topping can be frozen in an airtight container for up to 2 months. Thaw completely before baking.

>>> **Spice Level** To reduce the level of spice in this recipe, replace half of the jalapeños with diced green peppers. For extra spicy, stir in one diced fresh raw jalapeño along with the pickled jalapeños.

Penne all'Arrabbiata

This classic Italian dish is fun to pronounce, is simple to make, and has a blast of spice! Penne all'arrabbiata translates to "penne with angry sauce." It's angry, because it's spicy! A simple tomato sauce pasta is one of my ultimate home-cooking comfort-food favorites. Adding a ton of red pepper flakes gives a super spicy kick that I just can't get enough of! This sauce might be called angry, but for me, this sauce gives only happy feelings.

SERVES: 4	PREP TIME: 5 MINUTES	COOK TIME: 20 MINUTES	TOTAL TIME: 25 MINUTES

12 oz (340 g) penne or other short pasta (gluten-free if preferred)

2 Tbsp (30 mL) olive oil

4 cloves garlic, minced or pressed

1–3 tsp crushed red pepper flakes (see spice level)

1 can (28 fl oz/796 mL) diced tomatoes

¼ cup (60 mL) tomato paste

1 tsp white sugar

½ tsp salt

Sunflower Parmesan (page 107, optional)

Fresh basil leaves, torn (optional)

1. Bring a large pot of water to a boil and cook the pasta according to the package directions. Before straining the pasta, reserve ½ cup (125 mL) of the pasta water and set aside.

2. In a large skillet or pot, warm the olive oil over medium-high heat. Add the garlic and cook for about 30 seconds, until fragrant. Add the red pepper flakes and cook for 10 seconds more. Stir in the diced tomatoes, tomato paste, sugar, and salt. Bring to a simmer and cook for 15–20 minutes, until the tomatoes have cooked and the sauce has darkened in color and thickened slightly. If the sauce gets too thick, stir in the reserved pasta water as needed to thin it.

3. Toss the prepared pasta with the sauce. Garnish with sunflower parmesan and basil if desired. Serve hot.

>>> **Make Ahead** Allow the pasta and sauce to cool, then store in an airtight container in the fridge for up to 4 days. Enjoy cold, or gently reheat in the microwave or on the stove, adding a splash of water if needed.

>>> **Spice Level** If you like a *very* spicy pasta, I recommend adding the full 3 tsp crushed red pepper flakes, but my go-to is usually 1½ tsp. For those a little tentative about spice, I suggest starting with just ½ tsp crushed red pepper flakes, then stirring in more to taste once the sauce has cooked.

Spicy Peanut Noodles

Peanut noodles are one of my favorite lazy dinners for a rushed weeknight. But just because this dish is quick and easy doesn't mean that it needs to lack flavor! Creamy, salty, spicy—these noodles have it all! Use your favorite veggies in this dish to pack in the nutrition and add some delicious crunch.

SERVES: 4	PREP TIME: 15 MINUTES	COOK TIME: 10 MINUTES	TOTAL TIME: 25 MINUTES

FOR THE SPICY PEANUT SAUCE

½ cup (125 mL) natural peanut butter

½ cup (125 mL) water

3 Tbsp (45 mL) soy sauce (gluten-free if preferred)

2 Tbsp (30 mL) rice vinegar

1 Tbsp (15 mL) brown sugar

2 cloves garlic, minced or pressed

1 Tbsp (15 mL) minced or grated fresh ginger

2–3 Tbsp (30–45 mL) sriracha or similar hot sauce (see spice level)

FOR THE NOODLES

8 oz (227 g) vegan chow mein noodles or rice noodles

1 Tbsp (15 mL) sesame oil

Up to 4 cups (1 L) mixed raw veggies (such as snap peas, chopped red bell peppers, matchsticked carrots, shelled edamame, green peas, finely shredded cabbage, chopped green onions, chopped fresh cilantro, or frozen and thawed corn kernels)

¼ cup (60 mL) roasted, salted peanuts, coarsely chopped

Pinch of crushed red pepper flakes, for garnish (optional)

1. Make the spicy peanut sauce: In a medium bowl, whisk together the peanut butter, water, soy sauce, rice vinegar, brown sugar, garlic, ginger, and 2 Tbsp (30 mL) sriracha. Taste, and add the remaining 1 Tbsp (15 mL) sriracha if you like a spicier sauce.

2. Cook the noodles: Bring a large pot of water to a boil and cook the noodles according to the package instructions. Drain and set the noodles aside.

3. Return the noodle pot to the stove over medium-high heat, and add the sesame oil. When hot, add veggies of choice. Stir-fry the veggies, stirring often, for 2–5 minutes. You do not want to cook the veggies too much; you just want to warm them. Return the noodles to the pan, pour in the peanut sauce, and mix well. Serve with a garnish of chopped peanuts and crushed red pepper flakes if desired.

>>> **Make Ahead** Allow the peanut noodles to cool, then store in an airtight container in the fridge for up to 4 days. You can also prepare the sauce and any veggies in advance and store them separately in airtight containers for up to 3 days. When you are ready to enjoy, all you need to do is cook the noodles, stir-fry the veg, and combine with the sauce.

>>> **Spice Level** For extra spicy, add the full 3 Tbsp (45 mL) sriracha, or even more to taste if desired. For less spicy, use less sriracha, or you could even omit it for a non-spicy version.

Fiery Black Bean Soup

Hearty, spicy, and the perfect meal for a chilly day. This soup is great made ahead of time as the flavors get even better overnight. I love serving this soup with some avocado and a bowl of tortilla chips on the side.

SERVES: 6–8	PREP TIME: 15 MINUTES	COOK TIME: 33 MINUTES	TOTAL TIME: 48 MINUTES

1 Tbsp (15 mL) olive oil

1 yellow onion, chopped

2 ribs celery, chopped

1 large carrot, peeled and chopped

1 red bell pepper, chopped

6 cloves garlic, minced

3 cans (each 19 oz/538 g) black beans (about 6 cups/1.5 L), drained and rinsed

4 cups (1 L) vegetable broth or vegan beefless broth

2 tsp ground cumin

1 tsp chili powder

½–1½ tsp crushed red pepper flakes (see spice level)

1 bay leaf

½ tsp salt

2 Tbsp (30 mL) lime juice

OPTIONAL GARNISHES

Chopped fresh cilantro

Avocado

Tortilla chips

Lime wedges

Crushed red pepper flakes

1. Heat the oil in a large soup pot over medium-high heat. Add the onions, celery, carrots, bell peppers, and garlic. Sauté the vegetables, stirring often, until they begin to soften, 5–8 minutes.

2. Stir in the black beans, vegetable broth, cumin, chili powder, red pepper flakes, bay leaf, and salt. Bring the soup to a simmer and continue to cook for 25 minutes. Find the bay leaf and discard it.

3. Use an immersion blender to partially blend the soup until it is a bit thicker and creamier but there is still a ton of texture and whole black beans. If you do not have an immersion blender, you can use a standing blender. Ladle about 3 cups (750 mL) of soup into a standing blender and blend until smooth, being careful not to fill the blender too high so that your blender doesn't erupt. Return the blended soup to the pot and stir it back in.

4. Stir in the lime juice. Serve the soup hot with your desired garnishes.

>>> **Make Ahead** This soup is wonderful to make on the weekend and then enjoy all week long. Allow the soup to cool, then store in an airtight container in the fridge for up to 5 days or in the freezer for up to 4 months.

>>> **Spice Level** For a milder soup, use ½ tsp crushed red pepper flakes or even less. For spicier, go for 1½ tsp. I like the spicier version!

Lightning Ramen

This soup is quick to make, hot, and spicy, which is why I like to call it lightning ramen! Be prepared for this blaze of deliciousness. When I'm feeling a little under the weather, nothing makes me feel better than this ramen! Well, this soup, a cozy blanket, and a great rom-com. But you don't have to feel rough to enjoy this soup—it's scrumptious any day of the week!

SERVES: 4	PREP TIME: 10 MINUTES	COOK TIME: 16 MINUTES	TOTAL TIME: 26 MINUTES

1 Tbsp (15 mL) sesame oil

4 cloves garlic, finely minced or pressed

1 Tbsp (15 mL) minced or grated fresh ginger

8 cups (2 L) vegetable broth or vegan chickenless broth

1½ Tbsp (22 mL) white miso paste

2–4 tsp chili garlic sauce, plus more for serving (see spice level)

2 blocks (each 3 oz/85 g) dried ramen noodles (gluten-free if preferred)

4 oz (114 g) baby spinach

3 green onions, chopped (optional)

1 Tbsp (15 mL) sesame seeds (optional)

Soy sauce, to taste (optional, gluten-free if preferred)

1. Heat the sesame oil in a large soup pot over medium-high heat. Add the garlic and ginger and cook for 30–60 seconds, until the garlic just begins to brown and becomes fragrant. Add the broth, miso paste, and chili garlic sauce to taste (you can add more later if desired). Bring to a simmer and cook for 5 minutes.

2. Add the ramen and continue to simmer for another 5–10 minutes, until the noodles are cooked. Stir in the spinach to wilt. Serve hot with green onions, sesame seeds, more chili garlic sauce, and soy sauce if desired.

>>> Make Ahead I enjoy ramen freshly made so that the noodles are perfectly cooked and not too soggy. You can make the broth ahead of time and then cook the noodles fresh. The broth can be cooled and stored in an airtight container in the fridge for up to 5 days. Bring back to a simmer and proceed with the recipe from step 2.

>>> Spice Level For less spicy, use 2 tsp chili garlic sauce or even less. For very spicy, use the full 4 tsp chili garlic sauce and add more to taste when serving.

White Bean Tinga Tacos

These hearty, spicy, and smoky tacos are incredibly tasty! The sauce is easy to whip up and can be made ahead of time. I like mixing the sauce with white beans to make these spicy tacos, but you might just want to try drizzling this sauce on burrito bowls or dipping tortilla chips into it—it's delicious on everything!

MAKES: ABOUT 8 TACOS	**PREP TIME:** 10 MINUTES	**COOK TIME:** 21 MINUTES	**TOTAL TIME:** 31 MINUTES

FOR THE WHITE BEANS

- 1 Tbsp (15 mL) light oil (such as canola or vegetable)
- 1 yellow onion, thinly sliced
- 4 cloves garlic, minced or pressed
- 3–4 chipotle peppers in adobo sauce, chopped (see spice level)
- 2 tsp dried oregano leaves
- ½ tsp dried thyme leaves
- ½ tsp ground cumin
- 1 cup (250 mL) canned crushed tomatoes
- ½ cup (125 mL) vegetable broth or vegan chickenless broth
- ½ tsp salt (or to taste)
- 2 cans (each 19 oz/538 g) white beans, drained and rinsed

FOR THE TACOS

- 8 small flour or corn tortillas (gluten-free if preferred)
- Your favorite taco toppings (such as avocado slices, chopped fresh cilantro, chopped red onions, lime wedges, salsa, vegan sour cream, or lettuce)

1. Make the white beans: Heat the oil in a large skillet over medium-high heat. Add the onions and garlic and sauté for about 5 minutes, until the onions turn translucent and begin to brown. Stir in the chipotle peppers, oregano, thyme, and cumin and cook for 1 minute more to toast the spices. Stir in the tomatoes, vegetable broth, and salt. Cover, bring to a simmer, and cook for 8–10 minutes, stirring periodically.

2. Remove the sauce from the heat and transfer to a standing blender, or use an immersion blender. Blend until completely smooth and creamy. Return the sauce to the pan, stir in the white beans, and bring back to a simmer to heat the beans through, about 5 minutes.

3. Assemble the tacos: Serve the beans on the tortillas with your favorite taco toppings.

>>> *Make Ahead* Allow the sauce or beans in sauce to cool, then store in an airtight container in the fridge for up to 4 days or in the freezer for up to 4 months.

>>> *Spice Level* For less spicy, use just three chipotle peppers in adobo sauce and make sure to remove the seeds from the chipotle peppers before chopping. The seeds are the spiciest part. For extra spicy, use four chipotle peppers and do not discard the seeds.

>>> Now to the real meat of the book. I love meaty vegan recipes, and I can tell that many of you out there do as well, as the most popular recipes on my blog are vegan meat dishes! One of the reasons I fell in love with vegan cooking is because I realized I could make anything I wanted from scratch: eggs, cheeses, and, yes, even meat!

ME

ATY

In this chapter, I keep it simple with hearty mushrooms as a meat base. I show you my favorite meaty tofu hacks (which will make everyone love tofu). And then, the pièce de résistance, I include several recipes for homemade seitan! You're going to learn how to make vegan meats that are better than store-bought alternatives!

Mushroom Carnitas Tacos

Prepare for delicious savory aromas to fill your house and these meaty mushroom tacos to fill your belly. The mushrooms are thinly sliced and then baked in a blend of Mexican-inspired seasonings to make this luscious taco filling that is to-die-for delicious! Make sure you let these mushrooms bake long enough so that the edges of the pan start to burn—this will ensure that your mushrooms get a meaty texture.

MAKES: 6–8 TACOS	**PREP TIME:** 15 MINUTES	**COOK TIME:** 45 MINUTES	**TOTAL TIME:** 1 HOUR

FOR THE MUSHROOM CARNITAS

1½ lb (680 g) cremini or button mushrooms, thinly sliced (see note)

1 yellow onion, thinly sliced

½ cup (125 mL) orange juice (from 1–2 oranges)

4 cloves garlic, minced or pressed

1 Tbsp (15 mL) olive oil

2 Tbsp (30 mL) soy sauce (gluten-free if preferred)

1 tsp ground cumin

1 tsp dried oregano leaves

1 tsp smoked paprika

½ tsp black pepper

FOR ASSEMBLY

6–8 small flour or corn tortillas (gluten-free if preferred)

¼ red onion, chopped

1 small handful fresh cilantro, chopped

1 lime, cut into wedges

1. Preheat your oven to 425°F (220°C). Grease a large baking sheet (or two smaller baking sheets).

2. Make the mushroom carnitas: In a large bowl, combine the mushrooms, onions, orange juice, garlic, olive oil, soy sauce, cumin, oregano, paprika, and pepper. Toss well to evenly coat the mushrooms.

3. Evenly spread the mushrooms on the prepared baking sheet(s). Bake for 35–45 minutes, stopping to stir the mushrooms every now and then. About halfway through there will be a lot of liquid, but don't worry, this will dry up as the mushrooms continue to cook. Keep a close eye on them toward the end as the edges may begin to burn.

4. Assemble the tacos: Warm the tortillas according to the package directions. Fill the tacos with a heaping spoonful of the mushrooms, then top with red onions, cilantro, and a squeeze of lime (or any of your favorite taco toppings).

>>> **Make Ahead** Allow the prepared mushroom filling to cool, then store in an airtight container in the fridge for up to 4 days. Assemble the tacos fresh.

Note

Cremini or button mushrooms are great, but feel free to sub out the mushrooms for other varieties. King oysters, portobellos, or a mix of various mushrooms would be delish!

Sausage Bolognese

My favorite pasta before I became vegan was a tomatoey sausage sauce. I'm so pleased that I've been able to recreate this dish to taste even better than the original! The tofu is dried in the oven and then stirred into the sauce to make an amazing chewy texture, and the sautéed mushrooms add a juiciness. The pair make for the perfect meaty texture! But the key ingredient to this recipe is fennel seeds. Fennel seeds are commonly used in Italian sausage recipes—you will not believe how sausage-y this pasta tastes!

SERVES: 4–6	**PREP TIME:** 10 MINUTES	**COOK TIME:** 1 HOUR	**TOTAL TIME:** 1 HOUR 10 MINUTES

2 Tbsp (30 mL) soy sauce (gluten-free if preferred)

2 Tbsp (30 mL) olive oil, divided

2 tsp smoked paprika

1 block (12 oz/340 g) extra-firm tofu, drained (no need to press it)

1 lb (454 g) pasta of choice (gluten-free if preferred)

1 yellow onion, chopped

4 cloves garlic, minced or pressed

1 lb (454 g) mushrooms, finely chopped

2 cups (500 mL) Simple Tomato Sauce (page 165) or store-bought tomato sauce

¼ cup (60 mL) tomato paste

1 tsp fennel seeds

½ tsp black pepper

¼ tsp salt

Sunflower Parmesan (page 107)

Fresh basil leaves

1. Preheat your oven to 350°F (175°C). Line a large baking sheet with parchment paper.

2. In a large bowl, mix together the soy sauce, 1 Tbsp (15 mL) oil, and paprika. Add the tofu—you can either crumble it into the bowl with your fingers or use a potato masher to break it up into small crumbles. Stir to coat evenly in the marinade. Spread the tofu crumbles evenly across the prepared baking sheet and bake for 35–45 minutes, stopping to stir once or twice, until the tofu crumbles have browned and some of them are crispy. While the tofu is baking, you can move onto the next steps.

3. Bring a large pot of water to a boil and cook the pasta according to the package directions.

4. In a large skillet or pot, heat the remaining 1 Tbsp (15 mL) oil over medium-high heat. Add the onions and garlic and sauté until the onions soften and begin to brown, about 5 minutes. Add the mushrooms and cook them until they darken and begin to release their juices, another 5–10 minutes. Stir in the prepared tofu, the tomato sauce, tomato paste, fennel seeds, black pepper, and salt. Bring to a simmer and cook for another 5 minutes or so until the tofu has softened a bit. Serve with the hot pasta with a garnish of sunflower parmesan and basil.

>>> **Make Ahead** This sauce stores beautifully and gets even more delicious the next day. Allow it to cool completely, then store in an airtight container in the fridge for up to 3 days or in the freezer for up to 3 months.

Crunch Wrap Superior

CRAVINGS: CARBY, CHEESY, CRUNCHY, SPICY, MEATY
GLUTEN-FREE, MAKE AHEAD

Hearty, savory walnut meat is drizzled with queso cheese, then topped with tomato, lettuce, avocado, and jalapeño, layered with crunchy tortilla chips, and wrapped in a soft tortilla to make this crunch wrap. If that doesn't sound like comfort-food heaven, I don't know what does! This recipe has several elements to prepare, but everything is actually quite quick to whip up, so biting into this glorious creation doesn't have to be long from now!

SERVES: 4	PREP TIME: 15 MINUTES	COOK TIME: 16 MINUTES	TOTAL TIME: 31 MINUTES

FOR THE WALNUT MEAT

2 cups (500 mL) raw walnuts

½ cup (125 mL) sun-dried tomatoes (in oil), drained

1½ tsp smoked paprika

1½ tsp chili powder

1 tsp agave, maple syrup, or brown sugar

½ tsp garlic powder

½ tsp onion powder

¼ tsp salt

FOR ASSEMBLY

4–6 large tortilla wraps (gluten-free if preferred)

1 batch Super Simple Queso (page 89)

8 tostadas or about 24 tortilla chips

2 cups (500 mL) chopped iceberg or romaine lettuce

1 large tomato, chopped

1 avocado, mashed

1 jalapeño, thinly sliced (optional)

1. Make the walnut meat: Place the walnuts, sun-dried tomatoes, paprika, chili powder, agave, garlic powder, onion powder, and salt in a food processor. Pulse several times, stopping to scrape the sides as needed, until crumbly. Do not overmix it—you do not want this to be smooth; you want some crunch and texture.

2. Assemble the crunch wraps: Place a tortilla on a clean work surface. Pile one-quarter of the walnut meat onto the tortilla, then drizzle with a few spoonfuls of the queso. Place one tostada on top, or if you are using tortilla chips, place several tortilla chips on top, arranging them in a circle with triangle tops pointing in to make a single layer of crunch. Sprinkle with one-quarter of the lettuce and one-quarter of the tomato, dollop on some mashed avocado, top with slices of jalapeño, and then spoon on more queso. Repeat with the remaining ingredients to make four crunch wraps.

3. Fold the edges of the tortilla up and over the filling to make a flat, round pouch. If your tortilla is not large enough to cover the filling completely, then cut a circle from another tortilla, place it on top, and wrap your tortilla around it.

4. Heat a dry skillet (no oil) over medium-high heat. Working in batches, place one crunch wrap in the skillet seam side down and toast until golden brown, about 2 minutes. This will also seal the wrap closed. Flip and toast the other side for another 1–2 minutes, until golden. Enjoy hot with a drizzle of extra queso if desired.

>>> **Make Ahead** Make the walnut meat then store in an airtight container in the fridge for up to 4 days or in the freezer for up to 2 months.

Note

I like my Super Simple Queso recipe for this dish, but you can also try subbing my Cheddary Coconut Cheese Sauce (page 111), Roasted Red Pepper Cheese Sauce (page 114), or store-bought vegan cheese shreds.

Ginger Beef

CRAVINGS: SPICY, MEATY
MAKE AHEAD, FREEZER-FRIENDLY

You will not believe how meaty and delicious this beef seitan is! This recipe requires a few steps to make the seitan—make the dough, steam it, coat it in cornstarch, and then fry it—but every step is quick and SO worth the effort. The result is a crispy, beefy, sticky, gingery delight! Serve this over freshly steamed rice with a side of greens for an epic meal.

SERVES: 4	PREP TIME: 15 MINUTES	COOK TIME: 15 MINUTES	TOTAL TIME: 30 MINUTES

FOR THE SEITAN BEEF
¾ cup (185 mL) vital wheat gluten
¼ cup (60 mL) all-purpose flour
½ tsp smoked paprika
½ tsp onion powder
½ tsp garlic powder
½ cup (125 mL) water
1 Tbsp (15 mL) soy sauce

FOR THE GINGER SAUCE
3 Tbsp (45 mL) soy sauce
3 Tbsp (45 mL) brown sugar
3 Tbsp (45 mL) water
1 Tbsp (15 mL) rice vinegar
1 Tbsp (15 mL) minced or grated fresh ginger
3 cloves garlic, minced or pressed
1 tsp sesame oil
¼–½ tsp crushed red pepper flakes (optional for spice)

1. Make the seitan beef: Add about an inch (2.5 cm) of water to a pot with a steamer basket and bring to a light boil. Lightly grease the basket with a bit of cooking spray.

2. In a medium bowl, whisk together the vital wheat gluten, all-purpose flour, smoked paprika, onion powder, and garlic powder. Stir in the water and soy sauce to make a dough. You may need to mix the dough with your hand to ensure the flour is incorporated, but once the flour is mixed in, stop working the dough. You do not want to knead the dough, as the more you knead it, the tougher the vegan beef will be.

3. Tear small bite-size pieces of dough off and place them in the steamer basket. The dough will double in size, so I like to tear my pieces quite small for the perfect bite. Cover and steam for 10 minutes. Once the seitan is done steaming, remove it from the steamer and set aside on a plate. Let most of the steam evaporate from the seitan so that it dries off.

4. Make the ginger sauce: In a large glass measuring cup or a small bowl, whisk together the soy sauce, brown sugar, water, rice vinegar, ginger, garlic, sesame oil, and crushed red pepper flakes. Set aside.

5. Fry the seitan beef: Place the cornstarch and steamed seitan in a medium bowl or sealable bag. Toss or shake to coat evenly in the cornstarch.

RECIPE CONTINUES ⟶

MEATY 205

FOR ASSEMBLY

¼ cup (60 mL) cornstarch

2 Tbsp (30 mL) light oil (such as vegetable or canola), for frying

Cooked rice, for serving (optional)

2 green onions, thinly sliced, for garnish (optional)

1 Tbsp (15 mL) sesame seeds, for garnish (optional)

6. Heat the light oil in a large skillet over medium-high heat. Remove the seitan from the cornstarch, shake off any excess, and add the seitan to the pan. Fry for a few minutes per side until crispy golden brown, turning so the seitan is browned all over. Pour in the ginger sauce and cook for about 1 minute more, until the sauce has thickened slightly. Serve over a bed of rice with green onions and sesame seeds for garnish.

>>> **Make Ahead**   You can prepare the entire dish ahead of time, allow it to cool, then store in an airtight container in the fridge for up to 4 days. Seitan freezes really well, so I love to make a double recipe, steam it in batches, and then allow it to cool after steaming. Once cooled, store the batches in an airtight container in the freezer for up to 6 months. Thaw and then fry up fresh. Yum!

Seitan Steaks

What's meatier than a steak? Yes, you can be vegan and still enjoy a juicy steak dinner! This recipe comes from my blog and currently has a 5-star rating from over 250 reviews, so you know these are going to be good. Not only are these delicious, but they are actually really healthy for you as well! One of my vegan seitan steaks contains 295 calories, 42 g protein, 22 g carbohydrates, 4 g fat, 5 g fiber, 27.7% of the recommended daily iron intake, and 0% cholesterol. Pretty cool, right? I'm really not into numbers when it comes to food, but the fact that these steaks are both satisfying for meat cravings and are also super nutritious is just kind of awesome. Enjoy these steaks with Garlic Herb Potato Wedges (page 62) and a side of green veg.

MAKES: 4 STEAKS | **PREP TIME:** 10 MINUTES (PLUS MARINATING TIME) | **COOK TIME:** 35 MINUTES

TOTAL TIME: 45 MINUTES (PLUS MARINATING TIME)

FOR THE SEITAN STEAKS

1½ cups (375 mL) vital wheat gluten

1 cup (250 mL) cooked lentils (any kind—I use canned)

6 Tbsp (60 mL) water

2 Tbsp (30 mL) nutritional yeast

2 Tbsp (30 mL) tomato paste

2 Tbsp (30 mL) soy sauce

1 tsp garlic powder

1 tsp chili powder

½ tsp liquid smoke

¼ tsp black pepper

FOR THE STEAK MARINADE

¼ cup (60 mL) water

2 Tbsp (30 mL) olive oil

2 Tbsp (30 mL) soy sauce

1 Tbsp (15 mL) maple syrup or agave

1. Make the seitan steaks: Place the vital wheat gluten, lentils, water, nutritional yeast, tomato paste, soy sauce, garlic powder, chili powder, liquid smoke, and pepper in a food processor. Pulse to combine, stopping to scrape down the sides as needed, until everything is well mixed. Alternatively, if you do not have a food processor, you can first mash the cooked lentils with a fork or potato masher, then combine everything in a large bowl and mix well.

2. Turn the mixture out onto a clean work surface and begin to knead it together. It may be a bit crumbly at first, but keep kneading it for a few minutes until it comes together in a tight ball. Do not overknead the dough—the more you knead it, the tougher the steaks will be, so knead it just until it comes together. Cut the ball into four pieces, then use a rolling pin to roll out each section into ½-inch-thick (1.2 cm) steaks. The dough will be very tough and stretchy, but just keep working at it until you get your desired steak shapes.

3. Add several inches of water to a large pot with a steamer basket and bring to a boil. Put the steaks in the steamer basket and cover with a lid. It's OK if they overlap a bit. Steam for 25 minutes, flipping the steaks halfway through so they steam evenly. They will double in size.

RECIPE CONTINUES ⟶

4. Make the marinade: In a large sealable bag or airtight container, mix together the water, oil, soy sauce, and maple syrup. The oil won't really combine, but that's fine. Remove the steaks from the steamer and place in the marinade. Let marinate for a minimum of 30 minutes, or for as long as several days when kept in the fridge. Overnight is best. You can also freeze them at this stage.

5. Cook the seitan steaks: When you are ready to enjoy the vegan steaks, heat a frying pan, grill pan, or barbecue. When hot, brush the grill or pan with oil, and fry or grill the steaks a couple of minutes on each side until grill marks form. Brush the steaks with leftover marinade while cooking to keep them juicy, and also right before serving.

>>> **Make Ahead** These steaks are great for making ahead. I think they taste best when marinated overnight in the fridge or for up to 2 days. You can also freeze the seitan by popping the steaks in the marinade and freezing the entire thing, marinade and all, for up to 6 months. I have found that the steaks can suck up more of the marinade after they're frozen and thawed, so you might want to whip up extra marinade for brushing on when cooking. Fully cooked steaks can also be stored in the fridge for up to 4 days.

Red Lentil Pâté

This pâté is tangy, smooth, and salty and tastes just like the real thing! Lentils and sunflower seeds give this the perfect spreadable texture to use on crackers or bread, and it's incredibly healthy too. This recipe makes a big batch, so I like to divide the pâté into two—half to enjoy when I make it and half to freeze for later.

MAKES: ABOUT 4 CUPS (1 L)	**PREP TIME:** 10 MINUTES (PLUS CHILLING TIME)	**COOK TIME:** 15 MINUTES

TOTAL TIME: 25 MINUTES (PLUS CHILLING TIME)

1 Tbsp (15 mL) refined coconut oil

1 yellow onion, chopped

4 cloves garlic, minced

2 cups (500 mL) vegetable broth or vegan beefless broth

¾ cup (185 mL) dry red lentils

¾ cup (185 mL) raw sunflower seeds

2 tsp dried rosemary leaves

1 tsp dried thyme leaves

3 Tbsp (45 mL) melted refined coconut oil

1½ Tbsp (22 mL) apple cider vinegar

1½ Tbsp (22 mL) white miso paste

1½ tsp smoked paprika

¾ tsp salt

½ tsp black pepper

Crostini, fresh sliced baguette, or crackers, for serving

1. Melt 1 Tbsp (15 mL) coconut oil in a medium pot over medium-high heat. Add the onions and garlic and sauté until the onions turn translucent and begin to brown, about 5 minutes.

2. Add the broth, lentils, sunflower seeds, rosemary, and thyme. Cover and bring to a boil, then reduce to a simmer. Continue simmering for about 10 minutes, until the lentils are mushy and the broth has mostly been absorbed. If the lentils are not mushy but the broth has been absorbed, add a splash more if needed. If the lentils are mushy but there is unabsorbed broth, remove the lid and continue to simmer until most of the water has evaporated. Remove from the heat.

3. Transfer the mixture to a food processor along with the 3 Tbsp (45 mL) melted coconut oil, vinegar, miso paste, smoked paprika, salt, and pepper. Blend until as smooth as possible, stopping to scrape the sides as needed. I recommend blending for a long time to ensure it is extra smooth.

4. Spread the pâté into a serving dish. (The pâté will be quite liquidy before it sets). Cover and refrigerate until the pâté has completely cooled and has set, 4 hours or overnight. Serve with crostini, baguette, or crackers.

>>> **Make Ahead** Store in an airtight container in the fridge for up to 5 days or in the freezer for up to 4 months.

Note

Coconut oil firms up when chilled, so it is important to use coconut oil in this recipe to ensure that the pâté firms up.

Smoky Mushroom Meatballs

CRAVINGS: MEATY

GLUTEN-FREE, MAKE AHEAD, FREEZER-FRIENDLY

Crispy on the outside, tender and juicy on the inside, these mushroom meatballs are rich, smoky, and peppery. I love to enjoy these as a snack, as a nice appetizer, or served on pasta.

MAKES: ABOUT 20 MUSHROOM BALLS | **PREP TIME:** 20 MINUTES | **COOK TIME:** 20–35 MINUTES

TOTAL TIME: 40–55 MINUTES (PLUS CHILLING TIME)

½ cup (125 mL) dry brown rice or 1½ cups (375 mL) cooked brown rice

2 Tbsp (30 mL) olive oil

1 yellow onion, chopped

4 cloves garlic, minced

1 lb (454 g) mushrooms, coarsely chopped

½ cup (125 mL) breadcrumbs (gluten-free if preferred)

¼ cup (60 mL) all-purpose flour (gluten-free if preferred)

2 Tbsp (30 mL) nutritional yeast

1 Tbsp (15 mL) dried basil leaves

1 tsp salt

½ tsp black pepper

½ tsp liquid smoke

Light oil (such as canola or vegetable), for frying (optional)

>>> Make Ahead You can prep the balls ahead of time and store them, uncooked, in an airtight container in the fridge for up to 2 days. You can also store the fully cooked balls in an airtight container in the fridge for up to 3 days or in the freezer for up to 2 months.

1. If not already prepared, cook the rice according to the package directions.

2. Heat the olive oil in a large skillet over medium-high heat. Add the onions and garlic and sauté until the onions turn translucent and begin to brown. Add the mushrooms and sauté, stirring occasionally, until they release their juices and most of the liquid evaporates, 10–15 minutes. Remove from the heat.

3. In a food processor, combine the cooked rice, mushroom mixture, breadcrumbs, flour, nutritional yeast, basil, salt, pepper, and liquid smoke. Pulse several times, stopping to scrape the sides as needed, until the mixture is combined but there is still some texture. Take about 2 Tbsp (30 mL) of the mixture and form it into a ball—I like to use a cookie scoop to make it quicker and easier. Continue making balls with the remaining mixture, placing the balls in a single layer on a large plate. Cover and chill in the fridge for 1 hour or overnight before cooking for the best texture.

4. When ready to cook, you can fry, bake, or air-fry the meatballs.

Frying method: Fry the balls in a bit of oil on medium heat in a large nonstick skillet until they are browned all over, turning as needed.

Baking method: Preheat your oven to 400°F (200°C) and bake for 15–20 minutes, until golden and firmed up.

Air-fryer method: Preheat your air fryer to 380°F (193°C) and cook for 13–16 minutes, until they are golden and firmed up.

Chicken-Fried Tofu

CRAVINGS: CRUNCHY, MEATY
GLUTEN-FREE, MAKE AHEAD, FREEZER-FRIENDLY

Meaty, crispy, juicy, fried deliciousness—what more could you ask for? You can make the more traditional oil-fried version, or if you have an air fryer, you can whip up this dish with less oil. Enjoy this as the perfect bar-food snack or serve it with some Baked Panko Mac & Cheese (page 92), Crunchy Tahini Slaw (page 159), or Melty Mushrooms on Mash (page 124).

SERVES: 4	PREP TIME: 15 MINUTES	COOK TIME: 10–20 MINUTES	TOTAL TIME: 25–35 MINUTES

½ cup (125 mL) all-purpose flour (gluten-free if preferred)

2 Tbsp (30 mL) cornstarch

1 tsp salt

1 tsp smoked paprika

1 tsp garlic powder

1 tsp onion powder

2 Tbsp (30 mL) ground chia or ground flax

¾ cup (185 mL) warm water

1 block (12 oz/340 g) extra-firm tofu (optionally frozen and then thawed, see note)

1 cup (250 mL) panko breadcrumbs (gluten-free if preferred)

Light oil (such as canola or vegetable), for frying, or cooking spray, for air-frying

>>> **Make Ahead** This tofu is best enjoyed fresh, but leftovers can be stored in an airtight container in the fridge for up to 3 days. Gently reheat on the stove or in the air fryer.

1. In a medium bowl, whisk together the flour, cornstarch, salt, paprika, garlic powder, and onion powder. In another medium bowl, mix together the chia or flax and warm water. (If you are using chia, the mixture should thicken almost instantly. If you are using flax, let the mixture sit for about 10 minutes, until thickened.)

2. Tear the tofu in chicken tender– or nugget-size pieces. I like to tear the tofu instead of cutting it, as torn tofu has a much better texture and can grip the seasoning better.

3. Toss the tofu pieces in the flour mixture, shake off the excess flour, then set aside on a plate. Mix the panko into the remaining flour mixture. Now take the floured tofu and dip one piece at a time into the chia or flax mixture, and then into the flour and panko mixture. Repeat so all of the tofu is coated.

4. To cook the tofu, you can either fry or air-fry it.

Frying method: Heat about 1 inch (2.5 cm) of oil in a high-sided skillet over medium-high heat. When the oil is hot, use tongs to carefully place the tofu pieces into the oil. Working in batches, fry the tofu on one side until crispy and golden, about 5 minutes, then fry on the other side. Drain the tofu on a paper towel–lined plate and finish cooking the remaining tofu.

Air-fryer method: Preheat your air fryer to 380°F (193°C). Place the tofu in a single layer in the fryer basket, working in batches if needed. Generously spray the tops with cooking spray and air-fry for 10 minutes. Flip the tofu, spray with more cooking spray (making sure there are no dry spots), and continue cooking for another 10 minutes or so, until golden all over.

>>> **Make Ahead** The ribs can be prepared (steps 1–5) and then stored in the marinade in the fridge for up to 3 days or in the freezer for up to 6 months. Thaw and grill when ready to enjoy, brushing with extra barbecue sauce if needed. Cooked ribs can be covered and stored in the fridge for up to 3 days.

Rack o' Ribs

There aren't any bones in this rack of ribs, but aside from that, you'd be hard pressed to tell the difference. These ribs are made with vital wheat gluten to get that chewy, meaty texture. But the real secret here is that I add jackfruit shreds, which give that stringy pull-apart texture that is iconic with ribs, while still keeping them tender and chewy. YUM!

SERVES: 4	**PREP TIME:** 10 MINUTES (PLUS MARINATING TIME)	**COOK TIME:** 40 MINUTES

TOTAL TIME: 50 MINUTES (PLUS MARINATING TIME)

FOR THE RIBS

1 can (20 oz/567 g) young green jackfruit in brine or water, drained (about 1½ cups of shreds)

1½ cups (375 mL) vital wheat gluten

2 Tbsp (30 mL) nutritional yeast

1 Tbsp (15 mL) smoked paprika

1 tsp onion powder

1 tsp garlic powder

½ tsp black pepper

½ cup (125 mL) vegan beefless broth or vegetable broth

2 Tbsp (30 mL) soy sauce

½ tsp liquid smoke

FOR THE MARINADE

¼ cup (60 mL) water

3 Tbsp (45 mL) vegan barbecue sauce, plus more for brushing

2 Tbsp (30 mL) olive oil

2 Tbsp (30 mL) soy sauce

½ tsp liquid smoke

Note

You do not need the jackfruit cores or seeds, so you can either compost them or use them in Braised Cocoa Jackfruit Tacos (page 230) or Root Beer Pulled Jackfruit (page 218).

1. Make the ribs: Separate the shreds of jackfruit from the cores (the tough parts) and the seeds (see note). You will only need the shredded part of the jackfruit for this recipe.

2. In a large bowl, whisk together the vital wheat gluten, nutritional yeast, paprika, onion powder, garlic powder, and black pepper. Add the jackfruit, broth, soy sauce, and liquid smoke and mix to form a dough.

3. Turn the dough out onto a clean work surface and begin to knead it together until everything is combined. Bits of jackfruit will fall out, but that's ok. Work the dough just until everything comes together. The dough might look quite messy at this point, but everything will come together once it's shaped and steamed. Cut the dough into two or four pieces (depending on how wide your steamer basket is) and shape them into flat, rectangular rack of rib–shaped pieces that will fit in your steamer basket.

4. Add several inches of water to a large pot with a steamer basket and bring to a boil. Put the rib racks in the steamer basket and cover with a lid. It's OK if they are overlapping a bit. Steam for 30 minutes, flipping halfway through so they steam evenly. They will double in size.

5. Marinate the ribs: In a sealable bag or container, whisk together the water, barbecue sauce, oil, soy sauce, and liquid smoke. Place the steamed rib racks in the marinade and let marinate overnight in the fridge.

6. When ready to cook your ribs, heat up your barbecue or skillet and brush with oil. Cook the rib racks a few minutes per side, brushing with the leftover marinade to keep them moist, until both sides are brown and delicious-looking. Brush the ribs with extra barbecue sauce, then chop the racks into individual rib-size pieces and serve hot.

Root Beer Pulled Jackfruit

CRAVINGS: CARBY, MEATY, SUGARY
GLUTEN-FREE, MAKE AHEAD, FREEZER-FRIENDLY, ONE POT

This sweet, smoky, saucy jackfruit is similar to pulled pork, but in my opinion, way better! Adding a can of root beer to this recipe adds a ton of flavor while also making for sticky barbecue goodness. Serve this on a bun with a side of Crunchy Tahini Slaw (page 159).

SERVES: 4 | **PREP TIME:** 10 MINUTES | **COOK TIME:** 15 MINUTES | **TOTAL TIME:** 25 MINUTES

2 cans (each 20 oz/567 g) young green jackfruit, in brine or water (not in syrup!)

1 Tbsp (15 mL) olive oil

½ yellow onion, thinly sliced

4 cloves garlic, minced or pressed

1 can (12 fl oz/355 mL) root beer (1½ cups/375 mL)

1½ tsp liquid smoke

1 tsp smoked paprika

1 tsp ground cumin

½ tsp salt

½ tsp black pepper

½ cup (125 mL) vegan barbecue sauce (gluten-free if preferred)

4 hamburger buns or deli rolls (gluten-free if preferred)

Crunchy Tahini Slaw (page 159, optional)

1. Drain and rinse the jackfruit. Cut the jackfruit into smaller pieces by cutting it from the core to the edge for the most pulled texture (see page 14).

2. Heat the oil in a large frying pan or skillet over medium-high heat. When hot, add the onions and garlic and sauté until the onions are tender and beginning to brown, about 5 minutes. Add the chopped jackfruit, root beer, liquid smoke, paprika, cumin, salt, and pepper. Cover and continue to cook for another 8–10 minutes, until the jackfruit is soft enough that it can be mashed.

3. Using a potato masher, smash the jackfruit until it breaks apart and looks pulled or shredded. Stir in the barbecue sauce and heat through. Serve on a bun with the slaw, if desired.

>>> **Make Ahead** Allow the pulled jackfruit to cool, then store in an airtight container in the fridge for up to 3 days or in the freezer for up to 1 month. Thaw and reheat the jackfruit if desired, and assemble the sandwiches fresh.

Chili Con Carne

Did you ever think you would see a vegan chili without any beans in it?? OK, technically there are beans in this recipe, since tofu is made of soybeans, but this is in no way similar to any other vegan chili you've had. Anybody who claims that they don't like tofu will be absolutely blown away by this recipe!

SERVES: 6–8   **PREP TIME:** 15 MINUTES   **COOK TIME:** 50 MINUTES   **TOTAL TIME:** 1 HOUR 5 MINUTES

¼ cup (60 mL) nutritional yeast

3 Tbsp (45 mL) soy sauce (gluten-free if preferred)

2 Tbsp (30 mL) olive oil, divided

2 blocks (each 12 oz/340 g) extra-firm tofu

1 cup (250 mL) finely chopped walnuts

1 yellow onion, diced

4 cloves garlic, minced

1 can (28 fl oz/796 mL) diced tomatoes (fire roasted when available)

½ cup (125 mL) tomato paste

2½–3 cups (625–750 mL) water

1½ Tbsp (22 mL) chili powder

1 Tbsp (15 mL) ground cumin

2 tsp smoked paprika

¼–½ tsp cayenne

1. Preheat your oven to 350°F (175°C) and line two large baking sheets with parchment paper.

2. In a large bowl, mix together the nutritional yeast, soy sauce, and 2 Tbsp (30 mL) oil. Add the tofu to the bowl. You can either crumble it with your fingers or use a potato masher to smash the tofu into small crumbles. Stir the tofu to evenly coat in the seasonings.

3. Divide the tofu crumbles evenly among the two prepared baking sheets. Bake for 35 minutes, stopping to stir it halfway through. After 35 minutes of cooking, sprinkle the walnuts evenly over one of the baking sheets and continue baking both sheets for another 10 minutes, until the tofu is dried and golden brown. (Adding the walnuts at the end will toast them up a bit and make them more flavorful.)

4. In the meantime, heat the remaining 1 Tbsp (15 mL) olive oil in a large soup pot over medium-high heat. Add the onions and garlic and sauté for about 5 minutes, until the onions begin to brown. Stir in the diced tomatoes, tomato paste, 2½ cups (625 mL) water, chili powder, cumin, paprika, and cayenne to taste. Bring to a simmer and cook for about 15 minutes, until the tomatoes have darkened in color and the chili has thickened slightly.

5. Stir in the baked tofu and walnuts, bring back to a simmer, and cook for another 5 minutes to let the tofu absorb the liquids and soften a bit. If your chili is too thick, stir in another ¼–½ cup (60–125 mL) water as needed until you reach your desired consistency. Divide among bowls and serve hot.

>>> **Make Ahead** Chili tends to taste even better the next day! Allow the chili to cool completely, then store in an airtight container in the fridge for up to 4 days or in the freezer for up to 3 months.

Bangin' Bratwurst

I have two tricks that make this recipe perfect. The first is that I sauté onions and garlic in a generous amount of vegan butter. The onions absorb a lot of the butter, and when added to the dough they mimic the little fat speckles that you would find in a traditional sausage. The second trick is to loosely form the seitan into a sausage shape, then wrap it in foil. When seitan is steamed it doubles in size, so when wrapped in foil it expands into the space forming a sausage shape. It also becomes tight and compact and has a very similar texture to traditional sausage.

MAKES: 8 BRATWURSTS	**PREP TIME:** 5 MINUTES	**COOK TIME:** 45 MINUTES	**TOTAL TIME:** 50 MINUTES (PLUS COOLING TIME)

3 Tbsp (45 mL) vegan butter

1 yellow onion, finely chopped

6 cloves garlic, minced or pressed

¾ cup (185 mL) vegetable broth or vegan beefless broth

¼ cup (60 mL) tomato paste

¼ cup (60 mL) white miso paste

1 Tbsp (15 mL) brown sugar

1 tsp dried oregano leaves or ½ tsp marjoram leaves

¾ tsp salt

½ tsp lemon pepper

½ tsp liquid smoke

¼ tsp black pepper

⅛ tsp nutmeg

2 cups (500 mL) vital wheat gluten

8 sausage buns (check to make sure they are vegan)

Toppings of choice (like sauerkraut, mustard, grilled onions, ketchup, and relish)

1. Melt the vegan butter in a frying pan over medium-high heat. Add the onions and garlic and sauté for about 5 minutes, until the onions turn translucent and begin to brown.

2. Transfer the onion mixture along with all of the remaining melted butter into a large bowl. Add the broth, tomato paste, miso paste, brown sugar, oregano, salt, lemon pepper, liquid smoke, black pepper, and nutmeg. Mix well. Add the vital wheat gluten and mix to make a dough. Knead the dough to make sure it's all combined, but once combined, stop kneading. The more you knead, the tougher the sausages will be, so only knead as much as required to incorporate the vital wheat gluten.

3. Tear off eight pieces of aluminum foil that are each about 10 inches (25 cm) square. Cut the dough into eight equal-size pieces. Take one piece of dough and place it on a square of aluminum foil. Stretch the dough into a sausage shape (it will double in size once cooked). If any bits of onion fall out, just tuck them in with the dough. Loosely roll up the foil and twist the ends closed. Repeat with the remaining pieces of dough to make eight sausages.

4. Add several inches of water to a large pot with a steamer basket and bring to a boil. Once boiling, add the sausages to the steamer basket, overlapping if needed, and steam for 40 minutes. After steaming, remove the sausages from the steamer and allow to cool completely in the foil in the fridge—overnight is best.

5. Once cooled, remove the foil. They are ready to enjoy as is, or you can fry or grill them to finish. I like to grill mine and then serve them on buns with sauerkraut.

>>> **Make Ahead** Store the steamed bratwursts in a sealable bag in the fridge for up to 4 days (you can leave the foil on or remove it). Or just chuck the bag in the freezer for up to 6 months. Defrost before grilling them.

Note

If you prefer to avoid using aluminum foil, roll the sausages up in parchment paper, then roll the parchment-wrapped sausages in cheesecloth and tie the ends closed with kitchen string.

The Best Burger Ever

The meaty chapter wouldn't be complete without a burger. And not just any old bean burger. For this book, we need the cream of the crop, the meatiest vegan burger there ever was! These days it's pretty easy to find excellent vegan burgers in your grocery store, which is fantastic. But if you're more of a DIYer, with just 10 ingredients you can make burgers that are much more affordable and just as delicious (if not better). Make these ahead of time and store in the fridge or freezer until ready to serve. Then toss them on the grill or in a frying pan, and you're set!

SERVES: 6	PREP TIME: 10 MINUTES (PLUS OVERNIGHT CHILLING)	COOK TIME: 25 MINUTES

TOTAL TIME: 35 MINUTES (PLUS OVERNIGHT CHILLING)

1 large beet (7 oz/200 g), peeled and cut into chunks (about 1 cup/250 mL)

½ cup (125 mL) cooked lentils (I use canned brown lentils)

¼ cup (60 mL) soy sauce

3 Tbsp (45 mL) water

1 Tbsp (15 mL) natural peanut butter or any other nut or seed butter

1½ tsp onion powder

1½ tsp garlic powder

½ tsp liquid smoke

¼ tsp black pepper

1½ cups (375 mL) vital wheat gluten

6 burger buns (check to make sure they're vegan)

Toppings of choice (such as lettuce, onions, tomatoes, pickles, ketchup, vegan mayonnaise, mustard, relish, or vegan cheese)

1. Place the beets, lentils, soy sauce, water, peanut butter, onion powder, garlic powder, liquid smoke, and pepper in a food processor (see note). Pulse, stopping to scrape the sides as needed, until everything is mixed together into a mush. Add the vital wheat gluten and pulse, stopping to scrape the sides as needed, until combined into a crumbly dough.

2. Divide the dough into six portions and, using your hands, form into six burger patties. (You could alternatively make mini patties for sliders!)

3. Add several inches of water to a large pot with a steamer basket and bring to a boil. Once the water is boiling, add the burger patties to the steamer basket in a single layer without overlapping, working in batches if needed, or use layered bamboo steamer baskets if you have them (the burgers can become funny shapes if they are piled on top of each other). Cover and steam for 25 minutes.

4. Once steamed, the burgers will look kind of funny at this stage, but don't worry! Allow the burgers to cool completely, then cover and chill in the fridge overnight before serving. Chilling overnight ensures the best burger texture.

5. Once the patties are steamed and chilled overnight, you can basically treat them as if they were raw burger patties. Pan-fry them or grill them for a couple of minutes per side, until browned and heated through. Place on a bun and top with your favorite burger toppings.

>>> Make Ahead Once cooled completely, transfer the burgers to an airtight container and store in the fridge for up to 4 days or in the freezer for up to 3 months. Allow them to thaw completely before using.

Note

If you do not have a food processor, you could follow step 1 and blend everything—except for the vital wheat gluten—in a blender. Pour the beet mixture into a large bowl and then add the vital wheat gluten and mix by hand to form a dough.

LATY

>>> Chocolate comes from a bean, so naturally vegans love it. Ba dum dum tss! Chocolate has such an amazing flavor. It can be savory, it can be sweet, it can be dark and intense, or it can be light and playful. Whichever way you like to get your chocolate fix, I've got it covered in this chapter, starting with two savory chocolate recipes and moving into some sweeter options.

Baked Beans Mole

Smoky, spicy, chocolaty, rich, and hearty—these Mexican-inspired baked beans are next level! You can enjoy a bowl of these beans alone as a main, or they are wonderful served over rice, in a burrito, or with some crusty bread. This dish is somewhere between a chili and a stew, so it tastes even better the next day—hello, leftovers!

SERVES: 8	PREP TIME: 10 MINUTES	COOK TIME: 55 MINUTES	TOTAL TIME: 1 HOUR 5 MINUTES

1 Tbsp (15 mL) light oil (such as canola or vegetable)

1 yellow onion, chopped

2 bell peppers (any color), chopped

6 cloves garlic, minced or pressed

1 can (19 oz/538 g) black beans, drained and rinsed

1 can (19 oz/538 g) kidney beans, drained and rinsed

1 can (19 oz/538 g) pinto beans, drained and rinsed

1 cup (250 mL) salsa (medium or hot)

1½ cups (375 mL) vegetable broth or vegan beefless broth

½ cup (125 mL) chopped walnuts

2 oz (57 g) vegan dark chocolate, coarsely chopped

1 Tbsp (15 mL) smoked paprika

1 Tbsp (15 mL) chili powder

½ tsp salt (or more to taste)

1 handful fresh cilantro, chopped, for garnish (optional)

1. Preheat your oven to 375°F (190°C).

2. Heat the oil in a large Dutch oven or oven-safe pot. When hot, add the onions, bell peppers, and garlic and sauté until the veggies soften and begin to brown, 5–10 minutes.

3. Add the black beans, kidney beans, pinto beans, salsa, broth, walnuts, chocolate, smoked paprika, chili powder, and salt and stir. Cover and put in the oven to bake for 45 minutes, stopping to stir halfway through. When done, the bean mixture will be bubbling and slightly thickened. Serve in bowls with a garnish of fresh cilantro, if desired.

>>> Make Ahead This is the perfect make-ahead meal—it will get even thicker and richer as it rests! Allow to cool completely, then store in an airtight container in the fridge for up to 5 days or in the freezer for up to 6 months.

Note

1) Feel free to swap out this variety of beans for other types of beans you might prefer. 2) I love the added crunch the walnuts bring, but feel free to omit them or sub with an equal amount of pepitas (shelled pumpkin seeds).

Braised Cocoa Jackfruit Tacos

CRAVINGS: CARBY, MEATY, CHOCOLATY
GLUTEN-FREE, MAKE AHEAD, FREEZER-FRIENDLY, ONE POT

Jackfruit has the most incredible shredded texture that looks and tastes like pulled pork! Here I combine the jackfruit with tomatoes, cocoa, smoked paprika, and other spices to make a smoky, rich, meaty, full-of-flavor taco filling that tastes like it's been stewing for hours (though it secretly takes only 30 minutes to make. Shhhhhh!).

SERVES: 4–5	PREP TIME: 10 MINUTES	COOK TIME: 20 MINUTES	TOTAL TIME: 30 MINUTES

2 cans (each 20 oz/567 g) young green jackfruit, drained and rinsed

1 Tbsp (15 mL) light oil (such as canola or vegetable)

1 yellow onion, thinly sliced

4 cloves garlic, minced or pressed

½ cup (125 mL) vegetable broth or vegan beefless broth

1 cup (250 mL) diced tomatoes (canned or freshly chopped)

2 Tbsp (30 mL) cocoa powder

2 tsp smoked paprika

1½ tsp brown sugar

1 tsp dried oregano leaves

1 tsp chili powder

½ tsp salt

½ tsp black pepper

10 small corn or flour tortillas (gluten-free if preferred)

Salsa

Chopped avocado

Lime wedges

Chopped fresh cilantro

Hot sauce

1. Jackfruit usually comes in either coins or triangle-shaped pieces in the can. There is a tougher core and a flakier outside. For optimal texture, cut the core of the jackfruit into thin slices. This breaks up the tougher core as much as possible and makes for the best shredded texture. Do not discard the core or seeds; they are totally edible, and you would just be wasting precious jackfruit! Just chop up the seeds along with the rest of the jackfruit.

2. Heat the oil in a large skillet over medium-high heat. When hot, add the onions and garlic and sauté for about 5 minutes, until the onions have softened and begin to brown.

3. Add the jackfruit, broth, tomatoes, cocoa powder, smoked paprika, brown sugar, oregano, chili powder, salt, and pepper. Bring to a simmer and cook for 10–15 minutes, until the tomatoes are cooked and the jackfruit is softened.

4. Use a potato masher to break up the jackfruit into shreds. If any liquid remains, continue to simmer with the lid off until most of the liquid has been absorbed. Or, if it is a bit dry, add a splash more vegetable broth as needed. Serve hot on tortillas with salsa, avocado, lime wedges, cilantro, hot sauce, or any other favorite toppings.

>>> Make Ahead Allow the jackfruit to cool, then store in an airtight container in the fridge for up to 4 days or in the freezer for up to 2 months.

Chocolate Peanut Butter Bombs

Craving something chocolaty, caramelly, and peanut buttery? I mean, aren't we all? Stuff Medjool dates—which naturally have a caramelly taste—with peanut butter and salty peanuts and coat them in chocolate and you have the simplest but most scrumptious of chocolaty treats. This one is a go-to fave!

MAKES: 12 BOMBS	**PREP TIME:** 15 MINUTES	**TOTAL TIME:** 15 MINUTES

12 Medjool dates

2–3 Tbsp (30–45 mL) natural peanut butter

¼ cup (60 mL) roasted, salted peanuts, coarsely chopped

8 oz (227 g) vegan dark chocolate or chocolate chips

Note

1) If you do not have a microwave, you can melt the chocolate in a double boiler.
2) You can sub the peanut butter with your favorite nut or seed butter, and sub the peanuts with your favorite nuts or seeds. Almond butter with crushed almonds, cashew butter with chopped cashews, or sunflower seed butter with roasted sunflower seeds are some delicious options!

1. Use a small knife to carefully cut a slit down the length of a date. Use your fingers to remove the pit in the middle and discard it. Repeat with the remaining dates.

2. For each date, spoon about ½ tsp peanut butter into the cavity of the date and sprinkle about 1 tsp chopped peanuts.

3. Melt the chocolate in a microwave-safe bowl in 20-second increments, stopping to stir as needed. Remove from the microwave when just a few tiny pieces are not melted, and stir to finish melting. (This will ensure that you do not burn the chocolate.)

4. Line a baking sheet or plate with parchment paper. Using small tongs, two forks, or toothpicks, dip a peanut butter–filled date into the melted chocolate and gently turn it to coat. Place the chocolate-covered date on the prepared baking sheet, and sprinkle the top with some extra chopped peanuts. Repeat with all of the dates. Pop the baking sheet in the fridge or freezer until the chocolate is set. Enjoy!

>>> **Make Ahead** Store in an airtight container in the fridge for up to a week or in the freezer for up to 6 months.

Chocolate Chip Cookie Bars

CRAVINGS: CARBY, CHOCOLATY, SUGARY
MAKE AHEAD, FREEZER-FRIENDLY

A cross between a cookie and a cake, these bars are soft and chewy and taste just like the best cookie in existence! The secret to making these bars extra fluffy is to add 1 tsp vinegar. Wait! I know that sounds weird, but just trust me on this. The vinegar will react with the baking soda to help the bars rise and make them pillowy. These are enjoyable while still warm and gooey from the oven, but they freeze nicely as well.

MAKES: 16 BARS	**PREP TIME:** 10 MINUTES	**COOK TIME:** 25 MINUTES	**TOTAL TIME:** 35 MINUTES

1½ cups (375 mL) all-purpose flour

½ tsp baking soda

½ tsp baking powder

½ tsp salt

½ cup (125 mL) vegan butter, softened but not melted

½ cup (125 mL) white sugar

½ cup (125 mL) brown sugar

¼ cup (60 mL) plant-based milk (such as oat or soy)

1 tsp vanilla extract

1 tsp apple cider vinegar or white vinegar

1 cup (250 mL) vegan chocolate chips (see note)

Note

Not into chocolate chips? (Weirdo—kidding!) Try subbing the chocolate chips with equal amounts chopped walnuts, chopped pecans, or raisins.

1. Preheat your oven to 350°F (175°C). Line a 9-inch (23 cm) square pan with parchment paper, leaving extra paper over the edge of the pan so the bars are easy to lift out.

2. In a large bowl, whisk together the flour, baking soda, baking powder, and salt.

3. In a medium bowl, cream together the vegan butter, white sugar, brown sugar, plant-based milk, vanilla, and vinegar. Add the wet ingredients to the dry and mix well. Lastly, add the chocolate chips and stir to combine.

4. Spread the batter evenly into the prepared pan and bake for 20–25 minutes, until the edges begin to brown and the middle no longer looks wet. Allow to cool in the pan for at least 20 minutes before removing and slicing.

>>> **Make Ahead** Allow the bars to cool completely, then store covered at room temperature for up to 5 days, or transfer to a freezer-friendly container and keep in the freezer for up to 3 months.

234 CHOCOLATY

Chocolate Pudding Cake

This is a picture of love if I ever saw one. This cake is so amazing! It's warm, ooey, gooey, fudgy, and chocolaty, and it has a secret superpower—it makes its own chocolate sauce! You just pop it in the oven, and then when you take a scoop, you'll find all of these pockets of chocolate pudding sauce hidden right in the cake. So cool, not to mention crazy delicious! Serve this alone or with vegan vanilla ice cream.

SERVES: 9	**PREP TIME:** 15 MINUTES	**COOK TIME:** 35 MINUTES	**TOTAL TIME:** 50 MINUTES

¾ cup (185 mL) + ½ cup (125 mL) white sugar, divided

1 cup (250 mL) all-purpose flour

½ cup (125 mL) cocoa powder, divided

2 tsp instant espresso powder (optional, see note)

2 tsp baking powder

⅓ cup (80 mL) vegan butter or refined coconut oil, melted

½ cup (125 mL) plant-based milk (such as oat or soy)

2 tsp vanilla extract

½ cup (125 mL) brown sugar

1¼ cups (310 mL) boiling water or hot coffee (see note)

Note

1) The instant espresso powder enhances the flavor of the chocolate. If you don't have it or don't want to use it, you can skip it. 2) Just as the espresso powder enhances the flavor of the chocolate, using hot coffee instead of hot water will also enhance the chocolate flavor and will give the cake a mocha taste—yum!

1. Preheat your oven to 350°F (175°C). Lightly grease an 8-inch (20 cm) square pan.

2. In a large bowl, mix ¾ cup (185 mL) white sugar, flour, ¼ cup (60 mL) cocoa, instant espresso powder, and baking powder until combined. Add the vegan butter, plant-based milk, and vanilla and stir to combine. Don't overmix. Pour the batter into the prepared pan and use a spatula to spread the mixture evenly across the pan.

3. In another bowl, mix the remaining ½ cup (125 mL) white sugar, brown sugar, and the remaining ¼ cup (60 mL) cocoa powder. Sprinkle the sugar cocoa mixture evenly over the batter in the pan. Give the pan a shake so that the sugar cocoa mixture evenly covers the batter.

4. Pour the hot water over top of the sugar cocoa mixture. Do not mix. It will look like a puddle, and that's the way it should be. Bake for 30–35 minutes, until the center looks almost set. Let cool for 15 minutes before serving this warm.

>>> **Make Ahead** While you can enjoy leftovers of this cake, it is best made fresh as it will be gooiest while it's still warm. If you wish, you can do some of the prep work up to 2 days in advance. Make the cake batter (step 2), cover, and refrigerate for up to 2 days. Mix up the sugar cocoa mixture (step 3) and keep it in a separate bowl or container at room temperature. When you are ready to bake, assemble and bake the cake as instructed in steps 3–4.

Almost Instant Chocolate Mousse

Whenever I need a quick fix of chocolate bliss, this is my go-to recipe. It takes just 5 minutes to whip up, and you have an easy, homemade, creamy, chocolaty mousse. It's the perfect instant treat! The creaminess and fluffiness of the mousse come from cold coconut cream. When a can of coconut milk is chilled in the fridge overnight, the cream separates from the water, making it easy to collect and whip up into mousse. I always store a few cans of coconut milk in the back of my fridge so that I can enjoy this recipe whenever I need a chocolate fix.

SERVES: 2	**PREP TIME:** 5 MINUTES (PLUS CHILLING TIME)	**TOTAL TIME:** 5 MINUTES (PLUS CHILLING TIME)

FOR THE MOUSSE

1 can (13½ fl oz/400 mL) full-fat coconut milk or coconut cream, chilled in the fridge overnight

¼ cup (60 mL) cocoa powder

¼ cup (60 mL) powdered sugar

½ tsp instant espresso powder (optional to enhance the chocolate flavor)

Pinch of salt

OPTIONAL TOPPINGS

Dollop of vegan whipped cream

Fresh berries

Drizzle of peanut butter or other nut butter

Orange or lemon zest

Flaky salt

Shaved chocolate

Chopped walnuts, hazelnuts, pecans, or peanuts

Crumbled cookies

1. Open the can of chilled coconut milk, scoop out the cream on top, and add to a medium mixing bowl. Discard the leftover coconut water or save it to add to a smoothie or curry. Add the cocoa powder, powdered sugar, instant espresso powder, and salt to the bowl. Use a hand mixer or whisk to whip into a creamy smooth mousse. Enjoy right away with optional toppings or store in the fridge for later.

>>> Make Ahead Store the mousse in the fridge for up to 3 days. It will become even thicker as it cools. You can also freeze it for up to 1 month, which will make it almost like a firm ice cream!

Note

Different brands of canned coconut milk will have more or less coconut cream, and the cream can be smoother or firmer. I recommend testing out different brands to find the one that gives you the best yield and creamiest texture.

This mousse takes just 5 minutes to whip up— it's the perfect instant treat!

Brownie Walnut Cookies

CRAVINGS: CARBY, CHOCOLATY, SUGARY
MAKE AHEAD, FREEZER-FRIENDLY

Is it a brownie? Is it a cookie? It's BOTH! These cookies are chewy and fudgy and taste just like brownies with the crunch of walnuts. Yuuuuummmm. This recipe is simple to make, and that's a good thing, because you'll probably be making these again, and again, and again, and again . . .

MAKES: ABOUT 14 COOKIES	**PREP TIME:** 10 MINUTES	**COOK TIME:** 12 MINUTES	**TOTAL TIME:** 22 MINUTES

1 cup (250 mL) white sugar

¾ cup (185 mL) melted vegan butter

½ cup (125 mL) cocoa powder

¼ cup (60 mL) plant-based milk (such as oat or soy)

1 Tbsp (15 mL) ground chia or ground flax

2 tsp vanilla extract

½ tsp baking powder

½ tsp salt

1⅓ cups (330 mL) all-purpose flour

½ cup (125 mL) chopped walnuts (see note)

¼ cup (60 mL) vegan chocolate chips

Note

Sub the walnuts with chopped almonds or chopped pecans, or omit them if needed.

1. Preheat your oven to 350°F (175°C). Line a large baking sheet with parchment paper or lightly grease it.

2. In a large bowl, place the sugar, vegan butter, cocoa powder, plant-based milk, chia, vanilla, baking powder, and salt and mix until combined. Add the flour and mix until just combined. Lastly, stir in the walnuts and chocolate chips.

3. Scoop about 2 Tbsp (30 mL) dough and form into a cookie shape. The cookies will not spread much, so make each cookie the desired size and thickness. Bake for 10–12 minutes, until the edges appear set. Let cookies cool on the baking sheet.

>>> **Make Ahead** Store the cookies in an airtight container at room temperature for up to 6 days or in the freezer for up to 3 months.

Double Chocolate Espresso Tart

Only the most serious chocolate lovers are welcome! A crunchy chocolate crust is wrapped around a decadently rich, silky-smooth, espresso-infused dark chocolate filling and topped with fresh berries. Um, yes, I will have seconds, thankyouverymuch. This tart is bougie-baker-level good, but it's actually pretty simple to whip up and can be made ahead of time, so it's my favorite dessert to really wow someone.

SERVES: 8–12	**PREP TIME:** 10 MINUTES (PLUS 3 HOURS COOLING TIME)	**COOK TIME:** 20 MINUTES

TOTAL TIME: 30 MINUTES (PLUS 3 HOURS COOLING TIME)

FOR THE TART DOUGH

2½ Tbsp (37 mL) warm water

1 Tbsp (15 mL) ground chia or ground flax

½ cup (125 mL) vegan butter

½ cup (125 mL) powdered sugar

1½ cups (375 mL) all-purpose flour, plus more for dusting

2 Tbsp (30 mL) cocoa powder

¼ tsp salt

FOR THE CHOCOLATE ESPRESSO FILLING

1 can (13½ fl oz/400 mL) full-fat coconut milk or 1¾ cups (435 mL) vegan culinary cream

1 lb (454 g) vegan dark chocolate, coarsely chopped

1 tsp instant espresso powder (see note)

1 tsp vanilla extract

¼ tsp salt

OPTIONAL TOPPING

1 cup (250 mL) fresh berries (raspberries, blueberries, strawberries)

1. Preheat your oven to 350°F (175°C). Line a 10-inch (25 cm) tart pan with removable bottom with a circle of parchment paper.

2. Make the tart dough: In a small bowl, mix the water with the chia. Set aside to thicken for 10 minutes.

3. In a large bowl, cream together the butter and powdered sugar. Mix in the thickened chia mixture. Add the flour, cocoa powder, and salt and mix to form a thick dough.

4. Lightly flour a clean dish towel and place the dough on the towel. Roll the dough into a circle that is a few inches larger than your tart pan. Gather the sides of the towel and use the towel to help you gently flip the dough into the tart pan. If the dough breaks, it's totally OK! Just press the dough into place using your fingers, correcting any cracks and filling any holes. Cut off the excess dough around the edges and prick the bottom all over with a fork.

5. Bake for about 13–15 minutes, until the dough looks dry on top and has slightly pulled away from the edges of the pan. Place on a rack to cool completely.

6. Make the chocolate espresso filling: When the pie crust is finished baking, place the coconut milk in a medium saucepan and bring to a gentle simmer (do not boil it). Remove from the heat and add the chopped chocolate. Using a spatula, stir the chocolate into the coconut milk until it is melted together. Lastly, stir in the espresso powder, vanilla, and salt. Pour the chocolate into the cooled crust. Carefully transfer the tart to the fridge to cool until set, a minimum of 2–3 hours or overnight. Serve cold with berries on top, if desired.

Note

1) Espresso powder really enhances the chocolate, making this taste even richer, but you can omit it if you prefer.

2) If you like, you can make this recipe in multiple mini tart pans for mini chocolate tarts.

>>> **Make Ahead** This is an excellent make-ahead dessert. Allow the tart to set for 2–3 hours in the fridge, then gently cover and store in the fridge for up to 1 week.

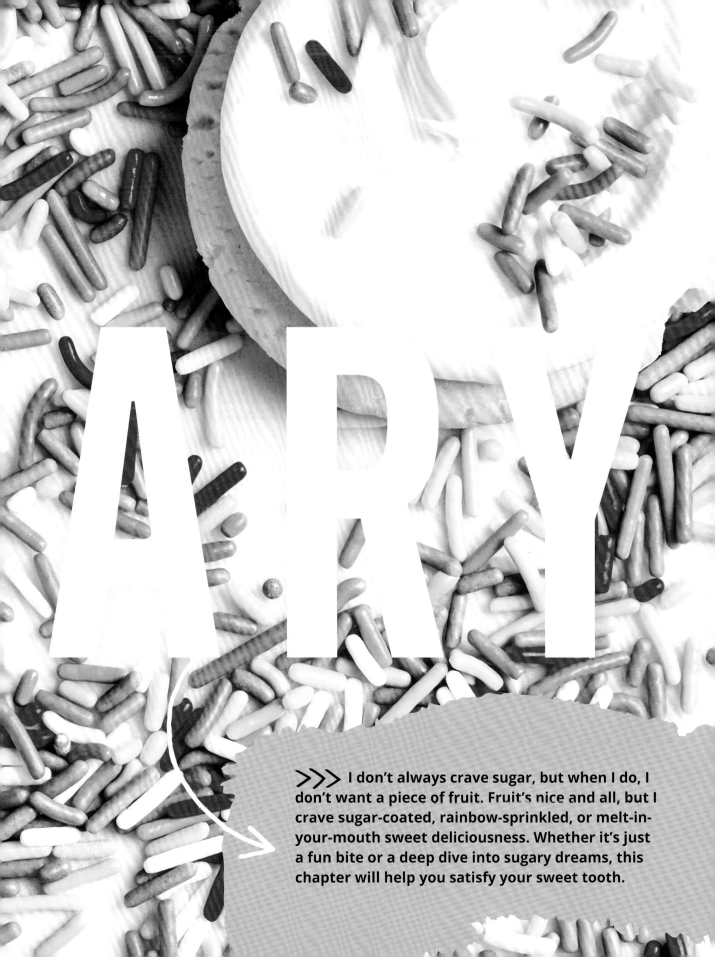

ARY

>>> I don't always crave sugar, but when I do, I don't want a piece of fruit. Fruit's nice and all, but I crave sugar-coated, rainbow-sprinkled, or melt-in-your-mouth sweet deliciousness. Whether it's just a fun bite or a deep dive into sugary dreams, this chapter will help you satisfy your sweet tooth.

Crispy Peanut Butter Cookies

My first cookbook has a recipe for peanut butter cookies that makes the classic chewier cookie, which is delicious, but have you ever tried crispy peanut butter cookies? No? Then you are missing out!! These cookies are baked at a lower temperature, which helps them get extra crispy. Every bite is deliciously crisp, sweet, melt-in-your-mouth bliss. Make sure to let the cookies cool completely for the ultimate crisp experience.

MAKES: 24 COOKIES	PREP TIME: 10 MINUTES	COOK TIME: 20 MINUTES	TOTAL TIME: 30 MINUTES

1 cup (250 mL) white sugar, plus more for sprinkling (optional)

½ cup (125 mL) vegan butter, softened but not melted

½ cup (125 mL) natural peanut butter (see note)

1 Tbsp (15 mL) plant-based milk or water

1 tsp vanilla extract

1¼ cups (310 mL) all-purpose flour

¾ tsp baking soda

½ tsp baking powder

1. Preheat your oven to 325°F (160°C). Line a large baking sheet with parchment paper or lightly grease it.

2. In a large bowl, cream the sugar and vegan butter together until light and fluffy. Stir in the peanut butter, plant-based milk, and vanilla. Add the flour, baking soda, and baking powder and mix until combined.

3. Roll the cookie dough into balls about 2 inches (5 cm) in size. Space out the dough balls on the prepared baking sheet and gently flatten, then use a fork to make a crisscross pattern. Optionally, you can sprinkle each cookie with a bit more sugar on top.

4. Bake for 17–23 minutes, until the cookies are lightly browned around the edges. Allow to cool completely on the baking sheet before enjoying. (The cookies will be soft when warm.)

>>> **Make Ahead** Allow the cookies to cool completely, then store in an airtight container at room temperature for up to 5 days or in the freezer for up to 3 months.

Note

Be sure to use natural peanut butter (the only ingredients in the peanut butter should be peanuts and maybe salt). The no-stir peanut butters are full of sugar and oil (they are basically icing). Natural is the way to go for the best peanuty flavor and the correct crisp texture! Feel free to sub peanut butter with your favorite natural nut or seed butter, such as almond butter, cashew butter, or sunflower seed butter.

Lovely Lemon Cookies

If you like lemon, you will LOVE these lovely cookies! They are crispy on the outside, with an almost caramel-like chewiness in the middle. They are bursting with zesty lemon flavor, hitting you with both very sweet and tart tastes all in one bite. They are an absolute delight!

MAKES: 18–20 COOKIES	**PREP TIME:** 15 MINUTES	**COOK TIME:** 11 MINUTES	**TOTAL TIME:** 26 MINUTES

1 cup (250 mL) white sugar

½ cup (125 mL) vegan butter, softened but not melted

2 Tbsp (30 mL) lemon juice

Zest of 1 lemon (see note)

½ tsp vanilla extract

1½ cups (375 mL) all-purpose flour

½ tsp baking powder

¼ tsp baking soda

¼ tsp salt

½ cup (125 mL) powdered sugar

Note

For a less tart cookie, simply omit the lemon zest.

1. Preheat your oven to 350°F (175°C). Line a large baking sheet with parchment paper or lightly grease it.

2. In a large mixing bowl, cream the sugar and butter together until light and fluffy. Stir in the lemon juice, lemon zest, and vanilla. Lastly, sprinkle in the flour, baking powder, baking soda, and salt and mix well to combine.

3. Spread the powdered sugar on a large plate. Take about 1 heaping Tbsp (15 mL) of the cookie dough and roll it into a ball. Now roll the ball in the powdered sugar to coat. Place the coated cookie ball on the prepared baking sheet and repeat with the remaining dough, spacing them out about 1 inch (2.5 cm) apart on the baking sheet so that they have room to spread.

4. Bake for 9–11 minutes, until the bottoms of the cookies just begin to brown. Allow to cool on the baking sheet for 10 minutes before removing.

>>> **Make Ahead** Cool the cookies, then store in an airtight container at room temperature, in the fridge for up to 1 week, or in the freezer for up to 3 months.

Sinful Cinnamon Buns

Cinnamon-swirled, pull-apart, carby deliciousness. As soon as I started writing this cookbook, I knew I had to include this fan-favorite sugary craving satisfier of a recipe from my blog. These cinnamon buns are the perfect sweet treat, and I designed this recipe to be as easy as possible too. No yeast. No rising. Only 10 ingredients. No hard-to-find ingredients. Freezable. Completely addictive!! No one will know they're vegan.

MAKES: 12 CINNAMON BUNS	**PREP TIME:** 35 MINUTES	**COOK TIME:** 28 MINUTES	**TOTAL TIME:** 63 MINUTES

FOR THE DOUGH

4½ cups (1.125 L) all-purpose flour

2 Tbsp (30 mL) baking powder

1 tsp salt

1 cup (250 mL) vegan butter, cubed

1¼ cups (310 mL) plant-based milk (such as oat or soy)

FOR THE CINNAMON SUGAR FILLING

¼ cup (60 mL) melted vegan butter

1 cup (250 mL) brown sugar

1 Tbsp (15 mL) cinnamon

FOR THE ICING (OPTIONAL)

1 cup (250 mL) powdered sugar

2 Tbsp (30 mL) cold vegan butter

1 tsp vanilla extract

3 tsp lemon juice or plant-based milk (see note)

1. Preheat your oven to 400°F (200°C). Lightly grease an 8 × 12-inch (20 × 30 cm) baking dish with sides or a 9 x 12-inch (23 × 30 cm) baking dish with sides, or line it with parchment paper. (To ensure you get soft, fluffy cinnamon buns, make sure to use the correct pan size. The buns should be touching in the baking dish before baking so that they expand into each other when they bake, keeping them tender. If there is too much air around each bun, they can end up getting crispy.)

2. Make the dough: In a large bowl, whisk together the flour, baking powder, and salt. Add the vegan butter and use a pastry cutter or fork to cut the butter into the flour until you reach a grainy texture. Pour in the plant-based milk and combine to make a shaggy dough.

3. Either in the bowl or on a clean work surface, use your hands to knead the dough together, incorporating any leftover dry ingredients until it all comes together into a nice ball. Let the dough rest in the bowl for 10–15 minutes for the best texture. Resting allows the dough to get stretchy, which is a must for gorgeous pull-apart cinnamon buns!

4. Roll the dough: Once the dough has rested, lightly flour a clean work surface and roll the dough with a rolling pin to create a 14 × 19-inch (36 × 48 cm) rectangle.

5. Assemble the cinnamon buns: Pour the melted vegan butter over the rolled-out dough and use a pastry brush or the back of a spoon to spread evenly over the dough. In a small bowl, mix together the brown sugar and cinnamon, then sprinkle the cinnamon sugar evenly over the melted butter.

RECIPE CONTINUES ⟶

I like using lemon juice in the icing to add a little bit of tang—similar to cream cheese frosting—but if you want an all-sweet icing, opt for plant-based milk.

6. Starting from a longer side of the dough rectangle, use your hands to gently roll the dough up. Once rolled, use a sharp knife and a gentle sawing action to cut 12 rolls. To ensure even-size cinnamon buns, I like to mark out each bun by lightly scoring the surface of the roll before doing the final cuts. Place the cinnamon buns in the baking dish, swirl side up.

7. Bake the cinnamon buns for 24–28 minutes, until puffed up and lightly golden. Let cool for 10 minutes before serving.

8. Make the icing (optional): In a small bowl, mix together the powdered sugar, vegan butter, vanilla extract, and lemon juice. Spread the icing roughly over the still-warm cinnamon buns. The icing will melt into the cinnamon buns a little. YUM!

>>> Make Ahead Cover and store leftover cinnamon buns at room temperature for up to 3 days, or store them (with icing and all) in an airtight container in the freezer for up to 2 months, then let thaw completely at room temperature. Cinnamon buns can also be prepared, cut, and placed in the baking dish (steps 1–6) and kept covered in the fridge for up to 2 days. When ready to bake, let them warm to room temperature for 20–30 minutes, then bake and frost following the recipe.

This old-fashioned pie is a classic for a reason—it's hands-down delicious!

Old-Fashioned Sugar Cream Pie

CRAVINGS: CARBY, CREAMY, SUGARY
GLUTEN-FREE, MAKE AHEAD, FREEZER-FRIENDLY

Is there anything better to satisfy a sugar craving than sugar pie? This delectable pie has a sweet, creamy, cinnamon-swirled, custardy filling with a tender, flaky pie crust. This old-fashioned pie is a classic for a reason—it's hands-down delicious!

MAKES: ONE 9-INCH (23 CM) PIE (8 SERVINGS) **PREP TIME:** 10 MINUTES (PLUS CHILLING TIME) **COOK TIME:** 45 MINUTES

TOTAL TIME: 55 MINUTES (PLUS CHILLING TIME)

1 unbaked Perfect Flaky Pie Crust (page 79), or frozen and thawed store-bought vegan pie crust (gluten-free if preferred)

FOR THE PIE FILLING
¾ cup (185 mL) white sugar
¼ cup (60 mL) cornstarch
1 can (13½ fl oz/400 mL) full-fat coconut milk or 1¾ cups (435 mL) vegan culinary cream
3 Tbsp (45 mL) vegan butter
1 Tbsp (15 mL) vanilla extract

FOR THE TOPPING
¼ cup (60 mL) white sugar
1 tsp cinnamon
3 Tbsp (45 mL) melted vegan butter

1. Preheat your oven to 325°F (160°C).

2. Bake the pie crust for 10–12 minutes to partially bake it. Remove from the oven and set aside.

3. Make the pie filling: In a medium saucepan, whisk together the white sugar and cornstarch. Add the coconut milk and stir to combine. Dollop the butter on top (the butter will melt into the mixture as it cooks). Set the saucepan over medium-high heat and cook, whisking often, until the mixture thickens, 5–10 minutes. Remove from the heat and whisk in the vanilla. Set aside.

4. Make the topping: In a small bowl, mix together the white sugar and cinnamon. Set aside.

5. Pour the prepared filling into the pie crust, filling it three-quarters full. Drizzle on the melted butter and evenly sprinkle with the cinnamon sugar. (If you have leftover filling, pour it into a container and pop in the fridge for a delicious pudding!)

6. Bake for 25 minutes. The pie will be bubbling and still very liquidy. Carefully remove from the oven and allow to cool on a rack at room temperature. Once cooled, move the pie to the fridge until set, about 3 hours, or overnight is best.

>>> Make Ahead Store the cooled and set pie covered in the fridge for up to 5 days. To freeze, wrap the pie tightly in plastic wrap and place in a freezer bag. It can be frozen for up to 3 months.

SUGARY 255

Super Simple Banana Pudding

This simple creamy pudding is a snap to make and totally satisfies my sweet fruity cravings. The pudding itself is mild and vanilla-y, so when the bananas are added, their flavor comes through! You can optionally top this pudding with a vegan whipped cream and any extra fruit or berries, if you wish.

SERVES: 4	PREP TIME: 5 MINUTES (PLUS CHILLING TIME)	COOK TIME: 8 MINUTES	TOTAL TIME: 13 MINUTES (PLUS CHILLING TIME)

¼ cup (60 mL) white sugar

¼ cup (60 mL) cornstarch

2 cups (500 mL) plant-based milk (such as oat or soy)

¼ tsp salt

Tiny pinch of turmeric (for color) or a few drops yellow food coloring (optional)

2 Tbsp (30 mL) vegan butter

1 tsp vanilla extract

1–2 bananas, sliced into coins (see note)

A few dollops vegan whipped cream, for topping (optional)

1. In a medium saucepan, whisk together the sugar and cornstarch until there are no lumps. Add the plant-based milk, salt, and turmeric and whisk to combine.

2. Set the pan over medium heat and bring to a simmer, whisking often. Continue to simmer for 5–8 minutes, until the pudding is slightly thickened and glossy-looking. It will thicken more as it cools. Remove from the heat and whisk in the vegan butter and vanilla.

3. Divide the pudding into ramekins, jars, or pudding cups, or pour all of it into a large bowl. Cover and let cool in the fridge for 3 hours or overnight, until chilled and thickened. When ready to serve, stir the sliced bananas into the pudding. Top with vegan whipped cream, if desired.

>>> **Make Ahead** Store the pudding in jars, pudding cups, or other sealable containers in the fridge for up to 5 days. Add the bananas just before serving.

Note

1) It may be tempting to add the bananas to the pudding while it cooks, but this makes the pudding brown and less tasty. Adding fresh bananas is the best for flavor and color. Just hold off on slicing them until the pudding has chilled.

2) Not into banana flavor? Try subbing with your favorite fruit or berries.

Melt-In-Your-Mouth Pralines

Perfect for the very sweet tooth! I enjoy these pralines on their own as scrumptious cookies, or I like to break one or two (or three or four) up and sprinkle them over plant-based vanilla ice cream for instant pralines and cream! Traditionally, pralines can be a more complicated recipe involving a candy thermometer, but this recipe is super easy—it's made with only six ingredients in 10 minutes, with no thermometer needed.

MAKES: 16–20 PRALINES	**PREP TIME:** 4 MINUTES (PLUS 30 MINUTES COOLING TIME)	**COOK TIME:** 6 MINUTES (PLUS 30 MINUTES COOLING TIME)

TOTAL TIME: 10 MINUTES

1 cup (250 mL) brown sugar

⅓ cup (80 mL) full-fat coconut milk, vegan culinary cream, or plant-based milk of choice

¼ cup (60 mL) vegan butter

1 cup (250 mL) powdered sugar

1 tsp vanilla extract

1½ cups (375 mL) pecan halves, toasted

1. Line a large baking sheet with parchment paper.

2. In a medium saucepan, whisk together the brown sugar, coconut milk, and vegan butter. Set over medium-high heat and bring to a boil. Whisking continuously, boil for 1 minute. The mixture should start to get foamy. Once it's foamy, remove from the heat and whisk in the powdered sugar and vanilla. Then mix in the pecans. Let cool slightly until it starts to thicken.

3. Use a spoon to scoop about 2 Tbsp (30 mL) praline mixture and dollop onto the baking sheet. Repeat to make 16–20 pralines. Let cool at room temperature for about 30 minutes, until completely set and cooled.

>>> **Make Ahead** Once the pralines are set and cooled, store them between layers of parchment paper in an airtight container in the fridge for up to 5 days or in the freezer for up to 2 months.

Birthday Cake Meltaways

When I have a craving for something sugary, I almost always want something birthday-cake flavored. It could be because of my nostalgic, dreamy, sugar-high memories of my childhood birthday parties, or perhaps I'm just drawn to the rainbow sprinkles . . . probably both. Either way, these sweet meltaway cookies satisfy my cravings every time. I love to keep a bag of them in the freezer so I can have a cookie whenever sugary cravings strike!

MAKES: 16 COOKIES	**PREP TIME:** 30 MINUTES	**COOK TIME:** 11 MINUTES	**TOTAL TIME:** 41 MINUTES

FOR THE COOKIES

1 cup (250 mL) vegan butter, cold

½ cup (125 mL) powdered sugar

1 tsp vanilla extract

1 tsp almond extract

1¼ cups (310 mL) all-purpose flour

½ cup (125 mL) cornstarch

FOR THE ICING

1½ cups (375 mL) powdered sugar

2 Tbsp (30 mL) vegan butter

1–2 Tbsp (15–30 mL) plant-based milk (such as oat or soy)

½ tsp almond extract

Few drops vegan food coloring (any color, optional)

2–4 Tbsp (30–60 mL) vegan sprinkles

1. Preheat your oven to 350°F (175°C). Line a large baking sheet with parchment paper or lightly grease it.

2. Make the cookies: In a large bowl, cream together the vegan butter, powdered sugar, vanilla, and almond extract until fluffy. Add the flour and cornstarch and mix well. Chill the dough in the freezer for about 15 minutes, until firm enough to handle.

3. Gently pinch off a bit of cookie dough and roll into a 1½-inch (4 cm) ball (roughly) or use a 2 Tbsp (30 mL) cookie scoop. Place on the prepared baking sheet and repeat with the remaining dough to make about 16 cookies.

4. Bake for 9–11 minutes, until the cookies are lightly golden on the bottom. Let cool on the pan completely before frosting.

5. Make the icing: In a medium bowl, mix together the powdered sugar, vegan butter, 1 Tbsp (15 mL) plant-based milk, almond extract, and food coloring (if using). If the icing is too thick, add the remaining 1 Tbsp (15 mL) plant-based milk, just a little at a time, until the desired consistency is reached. Use a butter knife or small spatula to frost the cooled cookies, then sprinkle with colorful sprinkles.

>>> Make Ahead Store the cookies once the icing has set. Arrange them on a plate and gently cover and store at room temperature for up to 5 days, or place in a freezer-friendly container and freeze for up to 6 months.

Acknowledgments

First, to my publishers at Appetite by Random House, Rachel, Robert, and the team, you have been nothing short of amazing throughout this process. Your guidance has been creative, caring, and always professional. I feel so honored that you have put so much trust in me.

To my friends and family, Mom, Dad, Emma, Gretty, Zuzu, Eleanor, Peter, Danielle, Al, and everyone else, thank you for your continued love and support and for always providing a vegan option. I love you all.

Thank you to my Adam and my Chickpea dog for being the best recipe testers (even though Chickpea is a little too picky). You are both my heart.

Thank you to my readers and everyone who makes up my amazing online community. It is your continued support that makes it possible for me to keep sharing vegan recipes.

To those who choose to satisfy their cravings the vegan way, thank you on behalf of the animals and our planet. This book is for you.

Index